TO BE OR NOT **TO BE**

TO BE OR NOT TO BE

Shedding an As-If Personality

STACY BLEMASTER

NAPLES, FL

Copyright © 2024 by Stacy Blemaster
All rights reserved.

Published in the United States by
O'Leary Publishing
www.olearypublishing.com

The views, information, or opinions expressed in this book are solely those of the authors involved and do not necessarily represent those of O'Leary Publishing, LLC.

The author has made every effort possible to ensure the accuracy of the information presented in this book. However, the information herein is sold without warranty, either expressed or implied. Neither the author, publisher, nor any dealer or distributor of this book will be held liable for any damages caused either directly or indirectly by the instructions or information contained in this book. You are encouraged to seek professional advice before taking any action mentioned herein.

All rights reserved. No part of this book may be reproduced or transmitted in any form by any means, electronic, mechanical, photocopy, recording, or other without the prior and express written permission of the author, except for brief cited quotes.

For information on wholesale orders or getting permission for reprints and excerpts, contact: O'Leary Publishing at admin@olearypublishing.com

ISBN: 978-1-952491-70-2 (print)
ISBN: 978-1-952491-71-9 (ebook)
Library of Congress Control Number: 2023921051

Developmental Editing by Heather Davis Desrocher
Line Editing by Kat Langerheim
Proofreading by Boris Boland
Cover and interior design by Jessica Angerstein

Printed in the United States of America

To all those struggling with mental disorders

CONTENTS

Foreword i

Introduction 1

Chapter 1 All That Glitters Is Not Gold 3

Chapter 2 Browned Off 23

Chapter 3 Dirty Little Secrets 29

Chapter 4 Locked Up 37

Chapter 5 The Rainbow of Color 51

Chapter 6 For The Love of God 61

Chapter 7 Recovery 77

Chapter 8 Married With Children 91

Chapter 9 Unbelizeable 111

Chapter 10 A Soulmate Makes Life Come to Life 115

Finish 125

Acknowledgments 131

About the Author 133

FOREWORD

This is the story of how one incredible woman overcame mental illness, using unconventional methods to live a full and joyful life. After many years of conventional treatment, Stacy found a way to rise above what held her back, using creative ways to live in the world. This is a deep dive into the interesting life of a fascinating and determined woman.

Stacy lived in a black-and-white, two-dimensional world, until she ventured to an Ivy League college – where her whole world changed and her mind was blown. When Stacy eventually experienced mania, she discovered a whole new, beautiful world. As you read her story, you will notice that her writing mirrors these contrasting worlds. She moves from a 2-D existence into a realm of color, filled with beauty and complexities. Stacy's description of the world of mania will entrance any reader. I hope you enjoy the world she shares!

To Be or Not To Be will inspire anyone who has struggled with mental illness – or those who love someone who has – to move through challenges and find what works specifically for them. The key, as Stacy discovered, is trusting one's own guidance system – while also using outside resources to help. While we cannot do it alone, we also have to take ownership of our journey. It is a balance that can take years to perfect – maybe even a lifetime. Hopefully, Stacy's story will inspire you to find more efficient ways to achieve such a balance, and can become one of the outside resources that helps you overcome your struggles so you can live a full and joyful life

Heather Davis Desrocher
Head Editor
O'Leary Publishing

INTRODUCTION

As humans, we are shaped by one another in profound ways. The first mold for who we are is our parents; particularly our mother. Our family of origin determines so much. And, of course, our parents are shaped by their parents – and so on, back through the generations. No one is perfect, but some parents do a better job than others at raising happy, healthy humans.

Many of us spend a large part of our life trying to recover from a job that was not done well. Our childhood is not something we can change while we are young – we're just not aware, or capable. This is not about blame, but about our awareness in adulthood that we can do something to change our lives and repair any damage that was done while we were children.

People seem to fall into one of two groups. First, there are those who hold onto their childhood, continuing to blame their parents, and letting that blame stop them from living life to the fullest. On the other hand, there are those who use their trauma or the wounds of their childhood to heal, evolve and create a good life – maybe even a life that they love.

In the end, who we become is a choice; and it is never too late to take responsibility for our life and how we want to live it. We come to this realization at different times and in different ways throughout our lives. My way has certainly been unique, and maybe yours has been too.

Things are not always what they seem. You may have grown up as I did – thinking one thing was going on, when it was something else. Many families keep dark secrets; mine sure did. Whatever the reason for the secrets (fear, guilt, shame), they cause illness and eventually come out in some undesired way. My story, like my family, has plenty of secrets. For me, secrets contributed to my mental disorder; but when I put them out in the open, they lead to healing and a life of love. So, I want to share them. Let me start at the beginning.

CHAPTER 1

ALL THAT GLITTERS IS NOT GOLD

1968-1987

Something very bad must have happened to Papa and Nana – my maternal grandparents – before they emigrated to Cleveland, Ohio, from Poland in 1929. I know this because I could never get any answers about my family history from my grandparents. Papa didn't say much; and when I asked Nana anything about her life in Poland, she would scream, "Shaw!" and spit on the floor. Any honest questions that family members didn't want to talk about were met with rationalizations that confounded me. Needless to say, school projects about my family were a bust. It was like the past didn't exist.

So, I know very little about what actually happened early on to my mother's family; but I believe there was some sort of abuse. I didn't realize it then, but with the experience of middle age, I see now that must have been the case. Things don't happen in a vacuum.

I loved Nana, and felt love from her (she used to tickle my back), but she was like a statue – asexual, austere and cold – most of the time. Her sister, Aunt Zelda, literally could not stop crying – ever. Nana and Zelda had lost their brother, Hyman, in World War II. They revered him, and often said, "He was so gorgeous!" I saw a black-and-white picture of him once. He looked nice, I guess.

When my grandfather came to the United States, he started a fruit stand that he later built into a $200 million real estate business. He was definitely the patriarch of the family. He made the money and held the purse strings. He was controlling and saw things in black and white. Things should be done in a certain way, according to Papa – it was his way or the highway.

He expected his sons to go to temple on the Jewish High Holy Days, Rosh Hashanah, and Yom Kippur. His children, as adults, were expected to spend only a certain amount of money on clothes, cars and houses. (This was all unspoken, but somehow everyone knew.)

CHAPTER 1

He was so rigid that he didn't visit his son and daughter-in-law for a year after they moved to a house in the country – because it was a house that he did not approve of (it was too far away and too expensive).

I had a very different experience with him. He was very kind to me and treated me like gold (befitting his Golderg name). My mother sat on his lap until she was 16 and I copied her behavior. I would run immediately to Papa as soon as I arrived at my grandparents' house. I was his favorite and we had a mutual understanding: we were both smart and on each other's wavelength. I always tried to impress him, especially when we played checkers and cards.

When I got married, he told my husband, "You got the best one." A day or two before he died, he pulled me aside and said, "You've brought me a lot of pleasure in my life." He was a man of few words.

Only one time did I see him angry, when he threw a mini Pac-Man game across the room. My cousin, brother, and I had wrapped toilet paper around the cars in his condominium complex in Florida on New Year's Eve. I can't say I blamed him.

I associated Papa with Abraham from the Bible. The Goldbergs reminded me of the Bible stories I learned as a child. I liked looking through the book on my grandparents' coffee table – a book about the Biblical family from Genesis. It was called *Wrestling With Angels: What Genesis Teaches Us About Our Spiritual Identity, Sexuality, and Personal Relationships* (Naomi H. Rosenblatt and Joshua Horwitz). I saw my family in those stories. My grandparents had two sons, Allan and Larry, like Abraham and Sarah had Cain and Abel. And my uncles fought just like Cain and Abel. My grandparents also had my mother, their youngest child.

My family seemed to be the center of the universe, just like the Biblical first family was the center of the universe in the Bible. I felt like God had given us privilege. We had lots of money, like they had lots of sheep. I sometimes wondered who I would be if I was in the Bible.

We had more money than any Jewish family in Cleveland, save two other families. Everyone seemed to know who I was, and I was given special treatment whenever people in the city found out I was a Goldberg. My mother told me that I could take any job I liked because I would be supplemented with a trust fund. I believed her and counted on that. I felt special.

My world was a world of wealthy, white Jews in middle America and it made me extremely proud. I thought we were the most privileged people on the

CHAPTER 1

Earth – more privileged than movie stars, or the president of the United States! Restaurants gave us their best tables. We occupied the most desirable houses in the city of Cleveland.

I thought we were the only ones to have fresh food! Of course, I noticed that fresh fruit and vegetables were en masse at the grocery store; but ours were better, somehow. Everything we had or did was better. I thought our family was especially good looking and that only good-looking people had sex. We were blessed.

There was a lot of competition between the 10 cousins in my generation. Like Joseph and his brothers – Jacob's sons from the Old Testament – I always felt like Joseph, Jacob's favorite. I felt that my cousins were jealous of me. It seemed I was praised more than any other cousin, except for maybe the eldest male cousin – *the doctor*. Were they disdainful of me? Were they picking up on my cutthroat competitiveness? I was brutal; I would even stand on my toes in pictures to be taller than any of them.

Needless to say, being around my cousins was very uncomfortable. I never felt like we were speaking the same language. Was I projecting my *own* insecurities on them? I felt no one was really honest about themselves, other than the Prada-wearing, Mercedes-driving, million-dollar-house-owning, Goldbergs. Anything that seemed like a weakness was hidden from not only the public, but also from each other in the family – and probably even from our *own* selves. It was like a game to see who could best pretend that nothing was bothering them. The women wore a lot of makeup, long perfectly-French-manicured nails, and simulated smiles on their faces. The men walked around in sport coats and patted each other on the back, as if it was a game of domination to see who could pat the other first.

On Jewish holidays, the men would start straightening their ties and looking at themselves in the mirror, ready to go to temple. Although I felt I was the most spiritual of them, I was afraid to ask to go, because it seemed to be a *male* thing. The family was misogynistic. When I summoned up the courage to ask if I could go, I was told, "yes," but everybody seemed perplexed and slightly annoyed. Women did not go to temple. They gave me patronizing approval about how nice it was that I wanted to go; but I suspected that no one was saying what they were really thinking. Breaking family protocol was frowned upon.

My immediate family, within the house I grew up in, was also fake. As in the extended family, everyone was supposed to always have a happy face. We never

CHAPTER 1

had conversations about anything other than how *great* things were going with academics, sports or friends. Discretion was important. It was discouraged to talk about unpleasant things, or feelings such as insecurity, anger, sadness or jealousy. My mother did not talk about sex or bodily functions. I don't think she wanted to be aware that any of us did something so disgusting as poop (there was no air freshener in the bathroom). I became very ashamed of my body and sometimes, I felt like an animal.

My mother would cook once in a while; but most duties were handed off to the housekeeper, Ann, who cooked our dinners and bathed us. We rarely had family dinners, and when we did, the tension was so thick you could cut it with a knife. My parents did not speak to each other. No one spoke freely. I thought it was normal to be disengaged from our parents. When my parents separated, my father would cook dinner for us in his apartment – or pretend to cook dinner. Later, we would find packaging from the gourmet food store in his garbage.

My mother did not seem very concerned about our safety. She spent most of her time on the phone. I don't remember her waiting for us to come home on the weekends when I was in high school. She never called my friends' houses when I would visit there to see if the parents were going to be home. When I brought beer onto the school campus in high school, breaking the rules and earning a suspension, my mom blamed the school. I was given a wide range of freedom and learned very little responsibility.

So, I never learned the reality of cause and effect during my formative years because there was no *disciplined* discipline. I was not held accountable in any rational or consistent way. I was threatened with a belt, but was never actually hit with one. I was threatened with huge, sweeping punishments like cutting off school or camp, but the threats were never enforced. And sometimes my mother would threaten to leave and never come back, which never happened either.

I think some people might wonder why I developed such an extreme mental illness. I did not look abused. I was not beaten. My pathology was created by fakeness – a fakeness that involved many little things that were not discussed, not enforced, and purposely fabricated to make the lives of my parents as easy as possible. When I tried to make sense of things over why my parents were making certain decisions (or later in life, when I began asking extended family members about my money), I always got a word salad.

CHAPTER 1

I don't remember much of my childhood. It feels like a mirage. I was not connected to my environment, because it didn't feel real. The falseness created an anger within me. I was angry with my parents, and eventually that anger turned inward (via depression), because my anger was not tolerable to my parents.

I was so scared of my mother that I failed to develop personal agency. I never developed an emotional balance that taught me how to advocate for myself. In the face of uncertainty or fear, I waited to react to others, because I never wanted to act out of line or offend anyone. I never felt in command of my own life. I used to stand speechless in front of my mother, afraid to move a muscle, for fear she would throw something at me. When I accidentally got ink on my mother's gold dress that she bought for my bat mitzvah, she went into a complete rage. I thought she was going to kill me. This was her normal response when something did not go her way. My mom called me a bad person and said that I should never have been born.

Unfortunately, I never saw my mother as a human being. I saw her as a concept: evil. When I was 13, my stuffed animal "doggie" that I had treasured since the age of 2 went missing. My mom said the new babysitter must have lost it. But for some reason, I always suspected that my mother took it, trying to wean me from it. She had always said, "What are you going to do when you get married? That animal can't sleep with you!"

Unexpectedly, I found it later, after I had become an adult. It was in her closet, ripped up. I asked her about it over lunch, but she had no explanation. She said with a smile, "Yeah, it was ripped up in my closet." Did she rip it up?

When I was 8 years old, I dressed up in high heels and makeup. My dad said I looked "gorgeous," but my mother gave me a dirty look. I felt I had done something horribly wrong. Was she jealous of me? Why didn't she say anything? I never dressed up that way again.

Years later, when I came home from college, looking for validation, I asked her if she ever had trouble deciding what to wear. She said, "No, never." I thought I must be the only one who had insecurities.

There was a reason my mother was the way she was. She was spoiled and treated like a princess all of her life. At age 15, when her family moved into their new house, she had a big round, white bed with fuchsia pillows – and her own dressing room.

CHAPTER 1

Everyone in her family treated her with kid gloves. I never saw my grandparents correct her. My grandfather managed her money until he died; then, her brothers took over. She wasn't interested in where the money came from, but she would express her displeasure when things didn't go her way. She was constantly offensive, and judgmental of other people. She would say whatever mean thing came to her mind – and I was a particular target. I would call my uncle and aunt, crying incessantly, asking for help; but they said they didn't want to interfere with another person's parenting.

I couldn't look to my dad for validation either. My dad comforted me one time, when she yelled at me about the gold dress, but that was the only time. Mostly, he was meek and just kept silent. Dad was easy-going – the "nice guy." He was the man-about-town, with slicked-back hair, a wide grin, and a twinkle in his eye. He was good looking, charming and charismatic.

The reason for my father's superficiality was that when he was 16, he had experienced a devastating trauma; his father killed himself. My grandma forged the death certificate, lying that he died of a heart attack in order to collect the insurance money. Six months after the death, she flaunted a new boyfriend. To this day, Dad says that her behavior is why he lives in denial. He is one who still holds on to his childhood.

My parents met at the swanky Hollywood, Florida, Fontainebleau Hotel while they were in college. Mom was attending Ohio State University and Dad was attending Hunter College in New York City. They were both in the "in-crowd." I think that was the basis for their connection – their popularity. She was charmed by his smooth New York ways. He was the kind of man to slip a tip to the maitre'd to get the best table; that impressed her Midwestern sentiments. But when they went off on their honeymoon, they got into a fight, and Mom threatened to get off the plane before it took off. My father said later that he should have let her get off the plane – he didn't, of course.

They moved to New York City, where my dad ran his family's hotel, but they promptly moved back to Cleveland because my mom didn't like it in New York. She missed her friends and family. Dad got a job working for Papa in Cleveland. Mom said they moved back to Cleveland because my dad wanted "an easy job, so he could play golf." Mom always said that she didn't respect Dad and was not impressed with the job he did for her father's business. She wanted him to "make more of himself."

CHAPTER 1

Dad had, and has, extreme attention-deficit disorder. He is still untreated. He can hardly pay attention to anything for more than 10 seconds at a time. In my childhood, he would look out the window as we talked, picking at his face. As with my mother, I felt unseen and unheard, and I concluded something was wrong with *me*.

Dad enhanced my life by encouraging competition, although it went too far. My father put a great deal of pressure on me to perform and win. He would race my brother and I outside on the lawn and in the swimming pool. Dad also coached me endlessly on spelling until I won a spelling bee. Praise was the way I felt love, so winning was important.

The year before I won, I actually cheated because I was so nervous that I spelled a word wrong. I went to the proctor and told him I forgot to fill in an answer on the preliminary written part. I erased and rewrote the correct answer, right in front of the proctor, with my head trying to cover what I was doing! It amazes me to this day that I thought he didn't notice. He didn't say anything at the time – I think he felt bad for me.

It helped that I was academically, athletically, and socially gifted. I sailed through childhood. I depended on my dad's love. Dad was affectionate, and I knew – even if he was compromised – that he loved me.

I did not feel love from my mother. She said she loved me, but the words always felt hollow. Although she bragged about my talents, she showed no awareness of my individual needs. I could never get a sense of who I was from my mother. I still feel that she sees me as someone other than who I am. All of her birthday gifts have always missed the mark; her gifts are things that *she* likes.

I have a brother, Steven, who is a year and a half younger than I am. Everyone calls him Stevie, which I find odd, because it makes him sound friendlier than he is. Stevie and I were comrades all throughout our childhood and he always followed me around. I was "the boss," a role I copied from my mother. I would set the rules for all of the games we played, especially Barbie (my favorite game); and often, I wouldn't let him play. I would never play army men with him.

I was resentful of my brother because he was mom's favorite, and I took it out on him. I was mean to him,

CHAPTER 1

and I even once pushed him down the stairs, causing him to need stitches. I felt horrible; but I didn't tell anyone, as I didn't want to get in trouble. I still owe my brother an apology. I'm sure glad I don't still have the ethical makeup I had when I was a child. I was a liar. But I often wonder what my relationship would have been like with my brother if my mother had not been the way she was.

When I was 10 and my brother was 8, the dynamic in our house changed. My mother and father came into my brother's bedroom while we were playing, and they said they had a big announcement. Mom was pregnant! This was the only time in my childhood I actually remember feeling joy. We were so excited, jumping up and down on the bed and feeling Mom's tummy – the magic of it all swirled in my head. I remember knowing at some point that it was going to be a girl, and we all debated whether she should be named Courtney or Allison. I liked Ali. We all voted for Allison.

Although I adored my sister, I no longer had any privacy. Before Mom got pregnant, we moved into a new house and I got to choose rooms. I chose the room closest to the bathroom. The only way to get to Ali's room was to go through mine, and people were constantly walking through my room. I begged to have the housekeeper's private room, but my mother refused. I was almost a teenager – desperately in need of privacy. I felt like I was on public display, even in my own room. I've read that it is a human being's right to be alone, but I didn't have that right. I wasn't even allowed to lock my door.

My father left when I was 13 and my brother was 11. I didn't know the specific reason for my parents' separation at the time, but I was glad about it because they never got along. It seemed the normal thing to do. At first they acted like it was temporary, which it was not. My dad moved to an apartment nearby, got remarried, divorced, and then moved to Florida two years later. My dad called me at camp to tell me he had moved.

My mother needed a male of her own to depend on, and so my brother Stevie became the man of the house. I was not really aware of the change in the family dynamic until later in life, when I saw my brother go from being my protege to my mom's partner in crime. The awareness surfaced in my adulthood when I realized he had taken control over the family.

CHAPTER 1

My childhood was a two-dimensional world. I was not in touch with my feelings and didn't share emotions. My parents' marriage was a sham. They were married on paper, but they didn't behave like a married couple. They never touched or kissed, or even said anything nice to each other. My mother yelled at my dad while he slept on the couch.

I didn't grow up knowing a functioning family life. Life was like being in a Barbie movie – surface-oriented. We pretended. Conversations didn't make sense, because my parents hid their weaknesses behind lies and shaming statements. I remember asking my mom once why the sky was blue, and the answer given was something like, "Why would you want to know that?" I could never get to the bottom of anything. I focused on image and achievement, and kept things private. Mostly, what I showed in public was haughtiness. I had to be the winner.

I often felt miserable, with no real connections to other people, even though I told myself that I was on top of the world. I cried a lot in my room; then I would leave my feelings there, with the tears on my pillow. I felt a great divide between my public persona and my private experience. I used grandiosity to cope and to cover up my insecurity. This is what Freud calls a *reaction formation*, when the opposite emotion takes the place of the real emotion. It was a defense mechanism and a way to make myself feel better.

Full of megalomania, I thought that not only was I the center of the Goldbergs, but also that I was the epicenter of the universe. I had it all figured out. The bottom line, as far as I was concerned, was that people seemed to like me. That made me think I was doing fine.

I had no idea that other people's lives were different from mine. I had no idea that they were living full, three-dimensional lives, with a spectrum of emotions, connections, and activities apart from me. They didn't share any of this with me. They were like caricatures to me, and they seemed to disappear when they weren't around me. My world was myopic.

Once in a while, when I heard that people I knew were hanging out with each other without me, I would think: *Maybe they're better friends with each other*. But I would immediately tell myself: *Given the opportunity, they would rather be with me*. I rationalized, which is another self-defense mechanism.

I was soon to discover that I was not who I thought I was, and the world "out there" was very different from

CHAPTER 1

the one I had known as part of the Goldberg family on the east side of Cleveland.

CHAPTER 2
BROWNED OFF

1987

In the fall of 1987, my world fell apart. My superficial personality had worked well in the east side suburbs of Cleveland, but it didn't work at Brown University. Things were simple and predictable in Cleveland. Everyone dressed the same. Everyone looked the same. Everyone spoke the same. There were rules. All one needed there was money, achievements and friends. In Cleveland, I checked off all the boxes.

I entered a new world of college, full of promise and optimism. But the transition from my two-dimensional world to the diverse, individualistic world of Brown University was a shock for which I was not prepared. By the second semester of my freshman year, I crashed emotionally. I couldn't get out of bed. I wanted to die.

I became a different person – a shell of myself. Everyone was shocked – most of all, me.

At Brown, I was out of my depth. I got my first clue of the impending devastation months earlier at my entrance interview, when my interviewer asked me what I was looking for in a school. I replied, "For people to be like me." He corrected me and said, "You don't want that. You want diversity." I was perplexed.

At Brown, there was no norm or clique to follow. I could not pick up on cues to follow from the environment. The lack of status quo was frightening. I did not do well with the individuality of others, because I did not have a healthy, integrated self. Of course, I had no understanding of that at the time. I just knew I could not cope. I couldn't understand how other people were functioning and making decisions. I was totally confused and overwhelmed.

I didn't know who to choose as friends; I didn't know what to say or how to behave. My days of fooling people were over. Brown students didn't grow up on the east side of Cleveland. I decompensated to the point where, in a depressed mood, my life was enveloped in pathology. My relationships with my best friend, Jessica, and my first love, Harris, relied heavily on discussions about problems. I had no ability to have ordinary conversations about day-to-day topics. I kept rationalizing to make myself feel better. Others were "too superficial," I would say to myself. They were wearing scarves. *Who wore scarves?* I never knew anyone in Shaker Heights who wore a scarf. And then I thought, *Should I try wearing a scarf?*

In my youth, *I* was the one who had been the trend setter. My socks always matched my clothes. I brought a matching pink Ralph Lauren bedroom set to college. I thought I was so cool. I thought I had it covered. My roommate, Allison, had hippie-like tapestries, randomly strewn across the wall. They were bleak and depressing. She wore no makeup, looked pale as a ghost, and had almost white hair. *Was she albino?* I was scared of her, like she might do something terrible to me while I slept. She was as bleak as her tapestries.

I have a vivid memory of crouching on the floor of my dorm room, telephone in hand, crying to my mother about my roommate. Allison was a "weirdo," I told her. I'm sure that Allison overheard me, but I was too self-absorbed to care. I am mortified now, remembering my behavior.

Three years later, during my senior year, I passed Allison on the street and talked with her. It was then that I realized I had missed a great opportunity to know a very cool person. I felt a feeling of loss and a sense of shame about my freshman attitude.

Throughout my four years of college, I kept my head above water by acting, on and off the stage. I had acted in theater my entire life – it's where I felt at home. Acting gave me a character to play – an identity. Brown was renowned for its theater program, and I fortuitously was cast as the lead in many plays.

I don't know how I kept it all together, remembering my lines and showing up on time. At one point, my boyfriend broke up with me, and I remember having so many stomach problems that I had to pause every 10 minutes in rehearsals to drink Mylanta. I always reverted back to my miserable self after a play ended.

At one point, my parents suggested I transfer to another college; but I was steadfast about sticking it out. I was determined to find out what was wrong with me. I was still intrinsically an overachiever. I could not let go of the opportunity to find out why I couldn't adapt to my environment. I was on a mission to reach my potential. More than that, I found some spirituality within me. It was my existential duty to my Higher Power to figure out my life.

CHAPTER 2

Looking back, I now see Brown University as a gift from God, because I collapsed so early in life. My experience at Brown gave me many years to recover and live an authentic life. Few people choose the more difficult path of self-exploration without life bringing them to their knees.

If I had gotten into Duke (which was my first choice), I might have joined a sorority of people "just like me" and gone about my superficial way for the rest of my life. My grades qualified me for entry into Duke, but I suspected that Duke didn't accept me because I had to say "yes" when they asked if I had been suspended from school. (Brown didn't ask.)

Brown University was like an atomic bomb to my personality. I took a class called Semiotics, which stressed that signs were signifiers of meaning, and taught that each of us had different connotations associated with the same word. There were multiple ways of viewing reality! I learned that my thoughts were crafted by the programming of other people and things (the culture, mainstream media, power structures). I realized that I was a mold. Fortunately, I found that I could break that mold; and when it did break, it cracked wide open and exposed my identity like it was jelly.

Toward the end of my senior year, I had dropped all my classes except for one. I was trying my best to graduate, but I took only the bare minimum number of credits. Now, I had no idea what I was going to do after college. I had failed to complete my auditions for a master of fine arts program in acting. I knew I would drown in the real world, and I dealt with that uncertainty by hiding in my apartment, binge eating, and having sex with a person who I did not know very well. He was 6-foot-5 and over 250 pounds – a water polo player. His large size helped me feel safe and protected. This situation cradled me in a holding pattern until I made a phone call to New York City.

CHAPTER 3

DIRTY LITTLE SECRETS

Spring 1991

While my family name was Goldberg, a more accurate family name might be Blackburn. We were a family of dark secrets, and it was at this time in my life, as I was finishing college, that I became more aware of the secrets.

Two weeks before I dropped out of college, I went to visit my childhood camp director for solace in New York City. He was another person who had chosen me as his favorite. He would hang out with me alone in his small cabin at camp (once he was showering) while my friends did normal camp activities. He was jealous when I spent time with other counselors; when I did that, he told me I was betraying him. He used to privately bring me gifts at camp and would fly to Cleveland to visit me. My parents were impressed with him; he had attended the University of Pennsylvania and Yale.

Unfortunately, the visit to New York City was not the solace for which I had hoped. He got me drunk and took advantage of me sexually. It felt like molestation, because I still felt like I was 10 years old when I was around him. And, the moment he touched me, it brought up fuzzy memories of molestation during my childhood by multiple family members. It started a decades-long process of uncovering sexual secrets, realizing deeper reasons for my pathology, and seeing my family for who they really are.

My hypothesis is that there is multigenerational sexual abuse in my family. It has manifested, in my opinion, in eating disorders and other dysfunctional, secretive behaviors. There are no signs of physical abuse. Verbal abuse wouldn't have been enough to create the issues I have observed. Only something as heinous as sexual abuse could have created so much of the dysfunction I saw in my extended family.

At one point, my mom accused my uncle (her brother) of sexually abusing her when she was a child. She kept the claim to herself until my aunt and uncle "usurped her authority" and took me to the hospital. But then, my aunt and uncle made the unseemly accusation go away as quickly as possible. They efficiently swept it under the rug, claiming that the whole family had discussed it, my uncle had denied it, and that they believed him. Within a few months, there was no more talk about it; and my mother, aunt, and uncle, completely composed by that time, were once again having dinner together. That was how they diverted their attention from the accusation. There was a slick veneer of overcompensation.

One motivation for sweeping things under the rug in my family is money. We all pooled our money together for large business ventures. That mattered more than anything, even sexual abuse.

Was my Nana sexually abused? She and my grandfather slept in separate beds. Was the origin of the dysfunction there, in their bedroom? There have been many sexual indiscretions in my family – affairs that sometimes even produced offspring. I blame it on repressed sexuality.

In my family, no one talks openly about sex. I believe that people who have healthy relationships with sex are able to talk about it, and are more disciplined with their sexual urges. The inappropriate behavior also happened surreptitiously. For example, certain males in the family hugged too long, rubbing children's buttocks.

I think the secret of sexual abuse leads to other secrets, and vice versa. When you have a big secret, you get used to lying or being duplicitous. I learned early on that speaking the truth was a bad thing. When I was 8, on vacation in the back of a van, I naively said, "You know what, Mom, you stutter!" The whole van went silent. No one responded and I felt like I had done something very wrong. It was obvious that although everyone else knew she stuttered, we were never to talk about it. No one ever did.

One of the bombshell secrets of our family was dropped on me when I was 17. I was studying acting at Yale University and my grandmother was dying of cancer in New York City. When I visited her that summer, she told me a secret while on her deathbed; I was never to reveal it unless absolutely necessary. My grandmother wanted someone to know that my mother had an affair and my sister was not my dad's child – which was the true reason behind the divorce.

CHAPTER 3

My grandmother was upset that my dad was being blamed for the divorce.

My sister was the product of a 10-year affair that my mother had with a family friend. We used to go over to this man's home when we were little. I remember that when my mother and father told us that Mom was pregnant, we were all so happy. As I look back, and realize what my dad must have gone through when he realized that my sister's blood type did not match his, the absurdity of all that time spent at that man's house becomes apparent.

My mother was speaking ill of my father at the time of their divorce and did not invite Dad to my sister's birthday party. Although my dad signed the paternity papers, my mother tried to turn the whole city against him (she had grown up in Cleveland – he had not).

My grandmother told me that I should not reveal the secret unless something drastic were to happen in the future (like my brother not inviting my dad to his wedding). I was to take care of my dad.

After I knew the secret, I felt I was doing wrong by my sister Ali by not telling her about her heritage. However, later, when I was in therapy, I learned that we are only as sick as our secrets. So, I decided I would not keep the secret anymore. I warned my mother that if she didn't tell Ali, I would. I was 23 at the time, Ali was 13. My mother told Ali the truth about her parentage – and I became very unpopular for a time.

When I dropped out of college and began serious psychotherapy, all of these things came to the surface. I had to reckon with my own troublesome relationship with my sexuality. With all the mixed messages concerning sexuality, I spent decades confused and shamed. I didn't allow myself to feel sexual as I related to other people. Sexuality was compartmentalized. I was unable to see people as sexual beings, which hampered my ability to see them as *human beings*. It contributed to the feeling of having a two-dimensional life. Sexuality didn't exist, unless it was the act of having sex and it was occurring in the present.

I see now that we are all sexual beings; sexuality lies at the heart of our essence. It is arguably the biggest part of our essence, and the biggest motivator for human behavior. It explains a lot of what we see going on around us. It is the subtext of a lot of conversation and behavior. Because of my denial of sexuality, I missed a lot of what was going on within TV programs or movies. Sex on TV or in the movies seemed surreal. I was disassociated.

Although I enjoyed sex, I recoiled at being touched in the most private of places. I felt it was too intensely personal, and wrong. I realized later I felt that way because it had been wrong earlier in my life. Feeling shamed sexually doesn't just come out of thin air.

Until I got my sexuality sorted out in my 50s, I had no chance of fully realizing a three-dimensional reality. But once I understood that sexuality is at our core, my world expanded exponentially. My awareness of sexuality erased a lot of my confusion; it helped me to shed my facade and become authentically human.

CHAPTER 4
LOCKED UP

Spring 1991 - Fall 1992

I tried psychotherapy and medication at Brown on and off for four years. My first psychiatrist, Dr. Kramer, was the author of the bestselling book, *Listening to Prozac,* so I felt a familiar "Goldberg" feeling of privilege, because he was famous. Due to being in denial, I was convinced at the time that I had a perfect childhood. However, when Dr. Kramer surprisingly broached the subject of my upbringing, my mother's "monster face" popped into my head. It was the face that had frightened me my whole life; I had always tried to put it out of my mind and pretend it didn't exist. In that instant, I knew immediately that something was wrong.

The moment that the face appeared before me in therapy, I had the feeling I was on the tip of an iceberg.

What lay beneath it? What else had I been ignoring? In a flash, I had the suspicious feeling that my whole life had been a lie. I panicked. I was not ready to investigate. I left therapy and decided to manage my issues using only medication, which was an insufficient substitute.

The universe, however, made sure that the Pandora's box of my life was about to open permanently. A book, *The Drama of the Gifted Child*, by Alice Miller, auspiciously crossed my path. Miller described the plight of the gifted child (an intuitive and bright one) as one who develops a *false self* to placate unstable parents. The child's real self goes unattended. The book rang so true to me. There was an explanation for my struggles – and I was not crazy!

Miller was ahead of her time. She didn't shy away from blaming parents. Mainstream psychology of the time mandated: *You must forgive your parents because they did the best they could.* A common trope referred to the Ten Commandments: *Honor thy father and thy mother.*

The psychoanalyst Donald Winnicott, along with Miller, insisted that parental environments, while not necessarily perfect, had to be *good enough*. The infant must be able to, calmly and non-threateningly, connect and then gradually individuate from the mother. This is how a baby integrates the environment with himself or herself.

I remember my mother giving me dirty looks whenever I would do something differently than she might have done. I remember walking away from her when I was 2 years old and looking back to see a mean face. I thought that it was wrong to do things on my own without her approval.

Without adequate support from the mother, the child will fail. I was one of those failures, and I was ready to be a standard-bearer for Miller's view of psychology, in which children should take their parents to task. There was some responsibility to be assumed.

I had failed multiple attempts at psychotherapy while in college, but the biggest failure was Cognitive Behavioral Therapy (CBT) during my senior year. I walked to my therapist's office five days a week, sometimes in the rain. I was very motivated, because I was suffering. However, the goal of this therapy – to help me recognize distortions in my thinking and to change my thought patterns – was not a good fit for me. I would spend hours writing down thoughts until they would blur together on the paper. I had so many thoughts racing through my mind that I couldn't grasp a single thought long enough to challenge it. Furthermore, how could I challenge a thought when I didn't comprehend reality? I was overwhelmed; I was desperate. The therapy experience led me to think hospitalization was necessary.

I had known a girl at Brown who had gone to a hospital for two weeks. That was what I wanted. However, my mother said she would not help me, because "hospitals are for people who can't get out from underneath the table." So I had lunch with my grandfather and begged him for help. I think he then asked my aunt and uncle to help me, because my aunt called me at college.

My aunt and uncle were an enormous help. They took me to a psychiatrist, who said I didn't need to go to a mental hospital (but if I wanted to, I could). I seemed to be the only person who knew how f-ed up I was. The psychiatrist presented three hospital options, and I chose the Menninger Clinic in Topeka, Kansas, because it was the farthest away from my family. Somehow, I knew that getting away from my family was essential.

CHAPTER 4

My parents did not react favorably to my hospitalization at the Menninger Clinic and tried to blame my camp director for everything. From the very beginning, my mother fought tooth and nail to get me out of the hospital. When she came to visit me, the most important thing to discuss – in her estimation – was that my car was dirty. The staff looked at each other and never invited her back again. They said, "We're going to have to do this without her."

My dad visited, but wasn't much help either. He lied about what really happened during my childhood, probably because he was fearful of being accused of sexual abuse. He used to over-cuddle with me when I was a child, often pulling me into bed with him. He told the Menninger staff that he wore a bathing suit when he brought me into the shower when I was a sick baby with the croup. I know my lazy dad; he would have never bothered to put on a bathing suit. Hospital inquisitions can be very unnerving for parents.

My mother would not agree to pay for my stay at the hospital. My father paid $80,000 for the first year of my hospitalization, while my grandfather picked up the rest of the whopping $300,000.

After the first two months in the Short Term Diagnostic Unit (STDU), I was given a "basket diagnosis": Borderline Personality Disorder (BPD). A basket diagnosis is commonly used when clinicians are not sure. BPD was in fashion in psychology in the early 1990s. Although borderline patients had a bad reputation among clinicians for being difficult to treat (they were thought to be temperamental, and split clinicians apart), I liked to think that *borderline* – in my case – meant that I was right on the borderline of being healed. That was how I shied away from the diagnosis and tried to de-pathologize myself.

Although I don't like to think of myself as a borderline, there is a great book about BPD called *I Hate You, Don't Leave Me* by Jerold J. Kreisman and Hal Straus. I *can* relate to it. I felt desperately dependent on other people at the time. I alternated between idealizing and devaluing them. The BPD person has trouble thinking of people having both positive and negative traits at the same time; a person is either all good or all bad. I was caught in that conundrum. I had another familiar trait of BPD – a *lack of object constancy*, which is the feeling that relationships don't exist when the other person isn't around. As a result, I often felt the BPD trademarks of emptiness and despair.

CHAPTER 4

There was a key event during my stay at Menninger Clinic that I will never forget – the moment that the world shifted on its axis – where things fell into place, and I was no longer the person I had been the moment before. I was sitting casually outside on a brick wall outside of the Short Term Unit when my psychiatrist Dr. Bellows-Blakely used the term *as-if personality*. I had never heard the term before, but the moment I heard it, I knew it was what I had. Finally, something somebody said made real sense.

This truth came as a great shock to me – that for my entire life, I had acted *as-if* I was Stacy! I did not feel like I was an *actual person* named Stacy! It was like I was acting in a play, reading off a script, or that I was a puppet controlled with strings by a puppeteer. I felt fake. I felt I did not belong. I was not an actual human being like other human beings. I was pretending. Bull's-eye – bingo – that was it!!

The term, *as-if personality*, likely originated from the psychoanalyst Helene Deutsch (1884-1982). It reminded me of Alice Miller's *false self*. Both terms, while not formal diagnoses in the Diagnostic Statistical

Manual of Mental Disorders (DSM), are jargon, denoting personality styles.

There are various definitions of *as-if personality*. The definition I have found that fits me best is from the American Psychological Association (APA) Dictionary of Psychology. It reads, "…a type of personality style in which the individual behaves as if well adjusted but, in fact, is doing only what is expected and is unable to behave in a genuine or spontaneous manner."

Instead of operating in the world, in the present, in reaction to other people, I was faking it. I would obtain a general reading of the room, and pick up ancillary clues as to what was happening. I developed prototypical ways of reacting and then used them as templates, over and over, in situations that felt similar. For example, if I saw a bunch of people praising me for something, I would say, "Thank you. Thank you so much!" If someone died or something bad happened, I would say, "I'm so sorry." I modeled others. Nothing extra, nothing improvised. I had developed a certain expected response for everything.

I did not know this was abnormal. I thought everyone was acting this way. Life felt like a script. It took me a very long time to realize that healthy individuals act more spontaneously – that people use their own language. We all are not the same. We all have different traits and ways of thinking about the universe. Although there is stability in our core, we are always evolving. I didn't know that my preferences meant anything significant. I thought they were accidental and random. Because of that, I looked at life as utter mayhem. There was no rhyme or reason, or patterns, or dependable outcomes – life was a confusing free-for-all.

The psychological literature does link *as-if personalities* with BPD. Clinicians seem to think that both conditions start with the mother, *the primary object*. So, because I didn't have a satisfactory relationship with my mother, I couldn't have a satisfactory relationship with *anyone*. That was why life made no sense. Life is about relationships. I had no real ones. There was a quotation in my senior yearbook that said, "If you aren't leaning, no one will ever let you down." It was like that song, "I am a rock, I am an island."

Marissa Moore, in her article, "*What is Quiet Borderline Personality Disorder?,*" describes the *as-if personality* as "quiet BPD," an unofficial term meaning "engaging with symptoms inwardly, instead of outwardly." Often, borderlines impulsively cut themselves, are addicted to drugs, are sexually promiscuous, and ragefully explosive. This was not me. I was passive-aggressive and well-mannered, but still internally felt the BPD extremes within me.

As-if personality and BPD were provisional diagnoses, but they landed me in the long-term unit where I spent a year and a half of my life. Most of the time I was in bed, crying to the walls that were hiding me in shame. Sometimes I was able to interact using my honed social skills, shooting the shit with others in the smoking room. But mostly I was in pain and isolated myself. I hardly left my room. I slept all the time. My private room protected me from the threatening faces and interpersonal dynamics on the ward. Every interaction seemed to trigger me and send me into anxiety. My recreational therapist bribed me with donuts in order to drag me out of bed to do wood-chopping therapy.

Who kept me going was my beloved long-term psychiatrist, Dr. Bauman-Bork. I remember when I first met her – I felt like God had placed her in my lap – the perfect mother I always dreamed of! She was soft-spoken, had long legs, perfectly curled blonde hair (with a curling iron), and a beautiful face. I had heard through the grapevine she was an expert with borderlines, and that they were all sent to her. No wonder! It takes a model person – loving, like her – to inspire trust from a person with BPD who feels frightened and guarded. I was in love with her, like an infant would be in love with its mother. She was empathetic. I always waited anxiously for her to visit the unit.

In a sense, she re-mothered me. In the womb of her office, I regressed back to an infantile state – fragile and vulnerable, latching onto her like a child with a breast. Kind and warm, she comforted and validated me. My deep, consistent relationship with her helped me with my issues of *object constancy*. It was much easier to attach to a face with soft features than to a "monster face."

She told me, "The good news is that your reality testing is intact." I've looked up *reality testing*. It means, "the objective evaluation of an emotion or thought against real life." She was telling me that I wasn't psychotic. I was in touch with reality, and therefore could – and did – challenge all of the nonsense I had been spoon-fed by my parents and extended family. Dr. Bauman-Bork would give me a reality check: "That wasn't very nice of your mother to do," she would say, while listening to a story about my childhood.

I had a good year with Dr. Bauman-Bork, but she abruptly left – without much more than a "goodbye"

— when she received a promotion to become the medical director of Menninger. She once told me she was *almost* perfect. I had believed her, but she wasn't perfect, after all. I felt abandoned.

She once told me that it takes people about 10 years after they're hospitalized to feel better. It took me *three decades*. I still miss her.

My next psychiatrist, Dr. Benarroche, told me that *no one* was perfect. "Perfect" didn't exist, he said. He tried to put my idealization of Dr. Bauman-Bork in perspective and ease my mourning.

One day, decades later, I found an essay online in which Dr. Bauman-Bork admitted to spending a lifetime trying – to no avail – to be perfect. She wrote that she regretted spending so much time thinking that she wasn't good enough for her husband. She used to say to him, "Don't you wish I looked like that woman?" We are all human, even those who can work miracles for others.

While my time at Menninger was difficult, it was also very healing and helpful. Under the auspices and care of Dr. Bauman-Bork, my *as-if personality* fell apart into a million pieces. The hospital served as a container for these pieces – it held me together. The hospital allowed me the freedom to avoid daily responsibilities, such as bill-paying, housekeeping, and car maintenance. I could focus on the feeling and healing of my emotions. On the other hand, and equally important, the rules of the hospital kept me from destructive behaviors like binge eating, drug use and casual sex. It also kept me from excessive isolation.

I was forced to be with other struggling patients in group therapy. It was very uncomfortable being stuffed into a small room with people who had tons of problems. I would see them yelling at the walls, or disheveled and chain-smoking in the smoking room. None of the patients ever had real conversations with one another; and then we would be forced to disclose personal feelings in a tiny room with a therapist. I always felt like the therapist looked at us like we were pitiful freaks. The intimacy of the room did help to break down my *as-if personality*, however. There was no hiding in that 6-by-6-foot room. I objected to being around "crazy" people in my locked unit. I told Dr. Bauman-Bork, "It is pulling me down." She responded with, "Being well means that you can be around any kind of person and not lose yourself."

Most importantly, the hospital kept me away from my toxic family and enabled me to model myself after well-adjusted caregivers. They did what they said they were going to do. They said what they meant. They meant what they said.

When Dr. Bauman-Bork left, I was transferred to Menninger Partial Hospitalization; the higher-ups in the hospital felt the transition would go smoothly. It was supposed to be a step up for higher-functioning patients. But I was devastated by the loss of my doctor. It was not smooth for me.

While I painfully mourned the departure of Dr. Bauman-Bork, what was about to happen to me would provide the missing piece I needed to get out of the hole I had been in for five years. Maybe there was something good about Dr. Bauman-Bork's departure after all.

CHAPTER 5

A RAINBOW OF COLOR

Fall 1992

I was walking around the partial hospitalization halfway house one day when I felt my energy begin to skyrocket. I had no idea what was happening. I thought I was becoming enlightened – that I was finally being rewarded for all the years of suffering in depression. I could feel tingles running up and down my legs and spine, like I had put my finger into a light socket or as if I had been struck by lightning. My thoughts were racing with vivid, elucidating images, which replaced the normal dull ones in my mind.

Almost instantly, everything appeared magical – colors were brighter – brilliant, even – and trees were a vivid emerald green. In my mind, I saw diagrams of the machinations of the entire universe – the patterns and meaning of each thing. Flashes of insight and understanding illuminated everything around me – interactions, behaviors and conversations. I felt like I could read people's minds. I was talking directly to God and receiving answers to all of my questions – instantly. As quickly as I could ask them, they were answered.

I felt like I was on a combination of psychedelic drugs and cocaine – both of which I had taken in the past. Psychedelics had revealed alternate and deeper meanings to me, while cocaine had boosted my energy and confidence. The combination I was feeling was magnificent. It was like watching black-and-white television for your whole life and then seeing a color television for the first time.

I wondered if everyone else saw life like this: *Am I the last to arrive or am I one of the enlightened few?* Questions raced through my mind.

Most importantly, for the first time in my life, an experience felt real to me – I wasn't pretending and other people weren't simply posing. The world seemed to come into focus, and I saw that everyone had a significant, purposeful role they were playing in life. There were no accidents. The world made sense on a very deep cosmic level. I was so relieved – life had felt so unfathomable and baffling before.

Then I wondered if I was delusional. My thoughts became even stranger. I had never thought about Jesus in my entire life, except as a vague cultural icon. All of a sudden, I sat at a restaurant believing that my friend was Jesus, and I started taking copious notes on cocktail napkins to witness his words. *Am I having a spiritual experience or am I going crazy?* Either way, I didn't ask anyone, because I felt intuitively that God wanted me to keep this experience private. I also didn't want anyone to lock me up. It was only after I saw another patient's face melt into a demon that I told my psychotherapist what I was seeing. I was scared. Dr. Athey said, "So, you don't think *you're* Jesus?" The lightbulb went on. *I* must be Jesus. I took that to mean he was telling me *I* was Jesus. All of this was leading to the next peak.

Now, *I* had meaning. *I* was a Christ figure who had endured decades of suffering, sacrificing my previous life to be born anew and to heal the world. I had a reason to be alive. More than that, the world made perfect sense now. I was overjoyed to realize God was in charge, and I was not a waste of breath on this planet.

I started believing that the staff at Menninger had known all along that I was Jesus and they were just waiting for me to realize it – for me to *arrive*. Previously, as I had wandered around Menninger's campus, I had thought about the elegant, stately collegiate buildings and I had felt like Menninger was some kind of peak-experience spiritual training ground for spiritual seekers.

Dr. Athey and I walked to the Partial Hospitalization Office, where I expected to be crowned as the Christ. Instead, they walked me back in a familiar direction, back to Inpatient Hospitalization. The door locked behind me. I was given loads of medication, which made it feel like my head was full of bricks.

My blissful feelings screeched to a halt. I was given a new diagnosis, bipolar disorder, and I was told that I was having a manic episode. I had never heard of this – all I knew was that I was locked up again and felt miserable. I had experienced a profound spiritual awakening, but they were calling it an illness.

As the whole thing dawned on me, I realized that now I could rethink my whole life. My experience of depression was only one side of the coin for me. Now there was another side of the coin: mania. I reevaluated everything I had gone through in my life through the lens of being a Christ figure – the favoritism, the overachievement, all of it. It seemed as though my parents were just the right parents to mold me, because I needed a fake mold to break in order to be reborn.

I had always thought of depression as an illness, but it was very hard to think of mania as an illness. *Are they both illnesses, or both real? Are they both illnesses and real?* Depression had made me feel that I had no hope; that the universe was a miserable place. Mania was a wondrous dream come true. The mania was so wonderful; it put depression in a new light. *Maybe you have to experience one to have the other!* There was a purpose to the depression, and it was *all* a spiritual path. My experience made me wonder about the things we call *good* and *bad.*

I have had other manic episodes since that first one, and I have always felt the same way about them: I feel blessed to see the spirituality in the universe.

Because of the intense, racing energy of mania, I opted to manage my manic episodes with medication until I could integrate those experiences into daily life all on my own. I did this for three decades. I think the process of enlightenment is so different; that its transposition on ordinary life doesn't meld seamlessly. I needed tools to moderate the energy.

I took a mood stabilizer (lithium) for two decades, along with an antidepressant (Luvox). Then I switched to a better mood stabilizer (Latuda) in my 40s (it first came out in the early 2000s). I learned to acknowledge when the medication wasn't holding, and to call my psychiatrist for an additional antipsychotic modification (Zyprexa) to flatten the curve of the intensity.

I didn't want to be like other manic-depressives I had heard about, who wouldn't take medication and never got their lives together. I can understand how bipolar patients want to hang onto the high, because it is so exciting. But I wanted both: the spiritual experience and a normal life.

I had crazy experiences that could have gotten out of control. In one manic episode, I took my dog across the country to see the guru, Carlos Warter, in Sedona, Arizona, with no money or credit cards. During that time, I danced in the pouring rain; bought myself flowers from God; put magical powers into my hands from hot tubs; and created artwork around a whole hotel room (crayons on sheets and walls). I also saw the clouds take the forms of cartoon characters. It is a good thing that my stepmother tracked down the driver I had hired to drive me around. My dad and my stepfather came to pick me up.

CHAPTER 5

In other manic episodes, I spent close to $100,000 on high-end, designer clothing. I was convinced that spending money helped stabilize my mania. In fact, I felt *ordered* by my Higher Power to make those purchases. Somehow, spending the money gave the energy an outlet. I felt I needed to buy things to keep the experiences from getting out of control. Fortunately, I had access to money. My ex-husband helped me out of debt by loaning me the money to pay off my Visa bill. Some bipolar patients get themselves into enormous debt.

When I contracted Bell's Mania (an extreme form of mania) in my mid-20s, I was incoherent. I was the most psychotic I have ever been; I was with my parents, who were worried that I would never come out of it, but my psychiatrist told them it would be temporary.

I was digging out grout between the bathroom tiles with a knife, metaphorically trying to eliminate old, outdated connections in my life. I spoke on the phone to my psychiatrist, who was in Argentina. I needed an extreme amount of antipsychotics, and it would be the most medication I ever took.

Medication has allowed me to get through the rough times – experiencing extreme mania is uncomfortable and scary. With a lot of scrutiny, I was able to figure out when I needed to feel some of the mania to increase my enlightenment, and when it was getting so high that I needed medication. The manic episodes decreased in intensity through my 40s. Now, in my 50s, I no longer have them.

Whether you consider it an illness or not, the experience of mania is real… and it is never forgotten. It has shaped the way I see life. Once I saw the brilliance and cosmic intelligence of this universe, life was never the same. Now, over the mellowing of many years, it has become my default perspective. Even when I have bad days and feel like I am losing my spiritual connection, I can always remind myself of the world of mania.

I decided after my first manic episode that, no matter what anybody said, I was never going to view myself as "sick." Being sick would lessen my worth as a human being and drain me of the energy I needed to get well. What could be sick about a reality as beautiful as this? I might have had an illness that needed to be managed, but I was not going to see it as something that was wrong with me. My illness is the culmination of a lifetime of experiences. It is both a capitulation to the abuse and a gateway to a better life. I believe all of those years of depression built up to a truth that needed to explode in my manic awareness.

CHAPTER 6

I choose not to be a victim. I traveled up to heaven in my mania and psychosis, found the knowledge I needed, and came back to earth with it, creating heaven on earth. It saved my life.

CHAPTER 6

FOR THE LOVE OF GOD

1992

I needed someone to help me live with my mania and get me situated in the world. I needed someone to believe in me. I wanted to believe I was a Christ figure – that there was meaning to my symptomatology – and that I wasn't sick. Not only did I need to believe in myself, but I also needed an advocate.

My parents were fed up with Menninger for misdiagnosing me for a year and a half. They felt that if the doctors had asked me the right questions, they would have realized that I had experienced a hypomanic episode – a lesser form of mania with elevated mood and disinhibited behavior – during my senior year of college. On that night, I had stayed up all night writing a screenplay (I wasn't a screenplay writer) and then ran multiple miles at dawn, which was highly unusual (I wasn't a runner either). If the staff at Menninger had known about that, they may have been able to put me on the right treatment path earlier.

The Menninger staff tried to keep me at the hospital, warning my parents that I would need to be institutionalized for the rest of my life. But my parents had me discharged. I went to Florida (where my father lived) instead of Cleveland, because I was too embarrassed to face people in my hometown. They had known me as a success; now I was a patient in a mental hospital. I was a failure.

Enter Dr. Cesar Benarroche. At this point, a thick scaffolding of my *as-if personality* had been dismantled at Menninger, and I was raw and vulnerable. I was scared that if I shared what I had just been through, I would face rejection. I sat in the office of Dr. Benarroche (he told me to call him Dr. B), my new psychiatrist at Fair Oaks Hospital in Delray Beach, and we read each other's minds. He was God to my Jesus. Dr. B walked onto the unit like he knew me.

Dr. B asked interesting, personal questions that no one ever had. He asked me if I saw pictures in my head. Nobody had ever asked me that; I was amazed.

CHAPTER 6

Somehow, he knew how I thought! He also asked me why I wasn't drinking caffeine. (I was secretly controlling my mania by drinking decaffeinated coffee, feeling privately powerful.) *How did he know that?* He hid a rock under a shell and asked me if the rock still existed. I said, "What's the point, if you can't see it?" He was knowingly pointing out my issues with object constancy. There was nothing I could hide from Dr. B.

Dr. B got into my head and earned my trust. Even more than Dr. Bauman-Bork, he understood me. He never told me that what I was now believing was wrong. He told me no one in my life would ever validate me as being Jesus, but I could believe it if I wanted to. He was successful with me because he was super-smart and direct. I would do anything he told me to do, since I trusted him.

He told me, "You're going to write a book." When I complained that I still wanted to be an actress, Dr. B said, "There's enough acting in real life." I was stunned, because I was not a writer. He said that I would be like the author Kay Redfield Jamison, who had written a book about bipolar disorder, *An Unquiet Mind*. She was a famous clinician with a best-seller. I revered her and I didn't think anything I could say would be worthy of her sphere of influence. Only "special" people could write books! But the idea stayed in my mind as a mandate, which I eventually fulfilled.

I was obsessed with this man. In my reverence for him, I gave him a poster of a drawing by M.C. Escher, which showed a complex set of machinery that appeared impossible to decipher or operate. It represented the thoughts in my head. I gave it to Dr. B because I wanted him to know that I had faith that He, as God, could even fix *me*.

At Menninger I was a "baby." In Florida, I grew into a "toddler." During the year and a half I spent at Menninger, I had regressed in my ability to take care of real-world responsibilities that I did not practice while I was there. But Dr. B told me to rent an apartment, buy a car and find a job. Because I felt overwhelmed, he gave me his pager number so I could contact him for every little thing. That's how I survived. Everything freaked me out, whether it was ants on the balcony or people flirting with me. I needed Dr. B to tell me how to act in each situation. He told me to buy Raid to handle the ants. (He drew the line at paging him about flirting, saying my call was not an emergency. He was good at boundaries.)

I spent three days a week in his office for sessions. I was still really suffering. I wished I was dead most of the time. The blissful mania was gone. I was back to spending most of my time in bed and binge-eating. I spent hours in my closet, trying to decide what to wear. I practiced shooting a gun at a shooting range, to see what it would feel like to shoot myself. I let my dog swim in a lake where there were probably alligators. I had a combination of mania and depression, which is referred to as "mixed episodes." I felt high and miserable at the same time.

Most of my difficulties were with other people. I brought Dr. B lots of fodder from my two jobs and pre-med classes at Lynn University. I was still lured by the power players (the beautiful and popular people of status), but I was figuring out that my place was with the humble people. It was a matter of meeting several different types of friends. I had failures and successes. It was all about trial and error; resilience and courage. There were no shortcuts.

I made a few good friends at the Florida subsidiary of Ohio Savings Bank, AmTrust Bank (owned by my cousins, who graciously gave me a job there.) I even went on a trip with them to Cocoa Beach, near where the space shuttle takes off, and shared some of my problems in a measured, honest fashion. They received me. Daringly, I remember taking the risk to tell my banker friend that I was scared of her pitbull. In the past, I would have been worried about offending. It was awkward, but good practice.

I was also friends with a stripper who dressed very sexy. It was a challenge for me to wear what was comfortable to me when I was around her – I was so used to mirroring. I summoned up the courage to dress differently from her, although I felt like a schlub. I preferred baggy jeans and T-shirts.

I had some friends who were patients at Fair Oaks Hospital. We talked about our problems until the boundaries of our illnesses became blurred. Dr. B told me to create distance from those people. Friendships should not be solely based on problems, he said.

I was intimidated by the snobby, popular clique at Chili's restaurant where I was a waitress. I found solace in a nice, quiet girl, with an unassuming boyfriend, who owned a pizza joint.

As I disclosed myself to Dr. B, and practiced disclosing myself to my peers, I gained some facility. Sometimes, what I said fell flat; sometimes I connected. It took a lot of work, chipping away continuously at my *as-if personality* and trying to find what was authentically *me*. Validation from others was helpful.

CHAPTER 6

Dr. B was my primary source of validation. He told me he knew Dr. Bauman-Bork because he had sent a patient to her at Menninger. *Was that patient me?* My head swirled with all the possibilities of how this man knew so much. I asked him to give me a book to read, to learn more about him. He gave me *The Good News About Depression*, by Mark Gold, a psychiatrist at Fair Oaks. It was a very clinical book, but I focused on the words "good news" in the title. I assumed that Dr. B was referring to the Good News from the New Testament. I was still Jesus.

I told Dr. B that I likened myself to the main character in Robert Heinlein's 1961 science fiction novel, *Stranger in a Strange Land*. The character was an alien. The stranger felt like he could *grof* (understand people in a different way than other people could). I could relate. I had always felt that I could sense or perceive what was going on inside people, and I confessed that to Dr. B.

Now, though, I attributed this *groffing* to the ability of Jesus. After a lot of thinking and trying to understand what had happened to me, I came to the conclusion that I must have been sent to this earth, to this Goldberg family, to help them reach salvation. I saw them as dysfunctional, status-seeking – and therefore, primitive.

They needed the wisdom that I had been courageous enough to attain. More than that, I felt I had been on a bigger mission. If I could heal my relationships with the Goldbergs, I would heal the world. I felt, as Stacy to the Goldbergs, I was Jesus to the evil in the universe. I could heal all at the same time.

The experience of mania brings lofty thoughts.

Most significant to my healing, I thought I was obsessed with good and evil because I was fixated on the good and evil within myself – what parts I had to get rid of and what I could keep. This was the major focus of my therapy. I remember complaining once to Dr. B that people who sped away after the light turned green annoyed me. He said, "Don't do it then." Dr. Benarroche seemed to have the smartest and wisest answers. The message was: *The only people we are in control of is ourselves.*

A "God" should also have healing powers, right? Dr. B used to press down his middle finger and turn it onto his desk as I talked about my mother. It was the weirdest thing I ever saw. I watched him do this right in front of me; he wasn't even trying to hide it. What popped into my mind was that he had special powers to heal me from my mother's evil energy. I thought it was so odd and that he might try to be more discreet.

I had always felt that I had taken on my mother's evil. It manifested itself in critical, cruel thoughts I had about others. It made me jealous, envious and mean. I used to behave inhumanely, yelling unabashedly at service workers when they were taking too long or if they got my order wrong. I was desperate to get rid of these traits. I felt I needed an exorcism or some other sort of supernatural healing to get a handle on them.

Dr. B, a looming figure, always put me in my place. Whether it was his strong, powerful Spanish accent, or his middle finger digging into his desk, I was humbled whenever I was around him. Grandiosity was a big part of my *as-if personality*. I confessed my biggest secrets (sins) to Dr. B (how could anyone keep secrets from God?). The most shameful secret I had was that I had touched my dog's genitals trying to figure out where the pee came from. I felt incredibly guilty; Dr. B told me to apologize to the dog.

The more bullshit I uncovered, the more authentic I felt. This was my reality-testing at work. In accordance with what Sigmund Freud wrote about, I was "recognizing the difference between the external and internal world." In telling my secrets to another human being, I was figuring out what was real and what was distorted from my upbringing. I was seeing what should be discarded.

The years with Dr. B also helped me with my object constancy. I was devastated when Dr. Bauman-Bork left me. But Dr. B really hung in there with me. I saw him over the course of two decades. I have less separation anxiety now when I am away from loved ones because of all the constant contact with Dr. B. I now trust that people will come back.

The self-disclosure and security helped in the further shedding of my *as-if personality*. I used to put on a good face when I was really feeling scared and alone. Now, I can go through the requisite feelings of loss. Dr. B witnessed all of my feelings – without judgment. Although he never told me I was right, he had a way of helping me feel comfortable in coming to my own conclusions.

I wish that all patients with personality disorders could have such a long-term, loving relationship. It takes time to do the re-parenting that is required for so many of us. Dr. B hung in there with me for so many years, for so many phone calls, for all of my needs, that he gave me faith that people continue to exist. He's dead now, but I still talk to him!

CHAPTER 6

I eventually had to leave Florida because the therapy with Dr. B came to a standstill. He had done what he initially said he was going to do; he had helped me to get on my feet and transition back into society, defying what Menninger had said. This man reintegrated me into life. He saved my life. He knew me better than anyone has ever known me.

On the other hand, my reverence for him had negative aspects. It involved an infatuation; a desire for a physical relationship that was left unrequited. I needed to get that monkey off my back. I needed to branch out to other people. I had childhood friends in Cleveland that I thought could provide a peer group, so I moved back to Cleveland. It was devastating to leave Dr. B, but I continued to travel to Florida and see him in the clinical setting whenever I felt the need.

I remember asking Dr. B when I was in my 30s, "What will I do without you when you die in 50 years? How will I even know?" He told me I would know. I figured he knew that because he was God. He said with a laugh, "You're worried about what's going to happen to me when I'm 80?"

He died in his 60's, much earlier than age 80. It was around 2103 and I was in my mid-40s. My father, who was also a patient of Dr. B, told me not to see Dr. B anymore, that he was sick and looked scary.

Dr. B did not look like himself because he was dying of cancer. I went anyway; I watched him wither away from a corpulent, vivacious man into a skeleton figure. I almost laughed at times when I looked at him, because I couldn't believe God could die. Now, I feel very guilty for laughing at a dying man. Hopefully, he forgives me.

Although I thought Dr. B was God, he wasn't the only one in my life that saved me – or the only one who used magic, for that matter. A therapist in Cleveland, Dr. Freedman, would wipe his face sporadically – but intentionally – when I discussed my inner conflicts. It was like he was symbolically wiping away and reorganizing my traumas as I spoke. It looked so choreographed that it looked funny, but he didn't try to hide it from me either.

I also had a teacher in graduate school, Kevin Prosnick, and his wife, Amy (who was my therapist at the time), sitting in class with me, twirling their feet in unison while I talked to the guest speaker. The guest speaker was very overweight, and I presumed that he had a lot of spiritual energy. As I pelted the guest speaker with questions, Kevin and his wife were doing these circular foot motions. I presumed they were trying to manipulate energy to facilitate the conversation.

After seeing those actions, it occurred to me that maybe you could heal someone by using ritualistic body motions while they struggled with their problems. It made sense to me, somehow. I have since adopted these practices myself. When I see a need, I sometimes try to heal other people with made-up hand motions. Whether the motions actually do manipulate energy or not, whether I heal people or not, at least I learned I could manage my own anxiety when I match a ritual (or behavior) with a troublesome feeling and then say a prayer. For example, if I secretly gave someone my middle finger, the threat seemed to go away. I felt like I was keeping evil away (a big focus in my life).

I think this may be the purpose of religious rituals – that performing a ritual feels empowering, like adding extra muscle to my prayers. I have used the strategy in my life with great results. I know that adding rituals or movements might sound unusual, but I have found that they work for me. I have never read anything about it, nor have I asked any of the doctors or teachers what they were doing when they were making those movements. I feel I am better off not really knowing because it seems a little spooky. And I don't want to be wrong.

Another unusual thing I began doing – and still do – is to attribute meaning to "random occurrences." As I pointed out, I wouldn't allow myself to think I was sick. So, in a psychotic state, while relentlessly focusing on certain things in my environment, I decided that repeated incidents must mean something. I felt God was always trying to tell me something, like with objects I saw in the road – like a random sock. I pretended that the sock in the street must mean something. I thought inwardly, *What could this mean? And why am I seeing it?* As I meditated on it, an answer pertinent to a life circumstance or question would come up for me. For example, maybe the sock would tell me that I needed to "cover up" and protect something in my life that I was leaving unattended. I remember when Dr. B asked me if the wood-grain pattern in the table meant anything. I said, "Yes." He didn't contradict me.

I also felt that messages came to me subliminally through what people were saying on the TV or singing on the radio. They seemed directed at me, and gave me a direction or an answer. I know the psychological profession considers things like these as symptoms of illness; but, for me, they were mechanisms that broke through to me with messages that I needed. As Shakespeare said, "There are more things in heaven and earth, Horatio, than are dreamt of in your philosophy." My *as-if* life was based on a very narrow view of the world – a world so small it could be on the tip of a needle. Mental illness created a haystack for that needle.

Mental illness, although painful, widened my world. Depression lowered my mood and created a whole new set of thoughts about the universe. I became more philosophical and detail-oriented. Depression made me obsessive, and caused me to ponder the meaning of existence and think about my place in the world. I questioned my presuppositions about the world I'd had since childhood. Everything was questioned – and perhaps, changed.

Mania showed me a world about which I could get excited. Once I could adapt to its energy, and slow myself down with medication, I was able to see more things in the universe that I had never realized. The world wasn't a horrible place where people were fake and controlling. There was a God who was in charge, and we were all co-inhabitants on a planet, perfectly designed for our evolution. Even more, we had more tools at our disposal for coping with that evolution than I had ever dreamed possible. In fact, we were co-creators!

I was soon to learn that there are actual steps – given to us by God, through a new friend, Bill W., and Dr. Bob – that are rules for life!

CHAPTER 7
RECOVERY

1996

I needed people in my world – for my sake, and for the sake of Jesus. I needed friends, and Jesus needed disciples. It took a while for me to get there.

When I returned to Cleveland, I entered a graduate program in counseling and human services at John Carroll University. I chose John Carroll over Case Western because it was a Jesuit university. This fit the bill for Jesus (although I couldn't relate to the hanging Jesus that was in each of the classrooms). The classes were not religious, but were taught by people who seemed to have faith – or who were at least spiritual. That was important to me at this point.

I remember watching the chipmunks run around one day on campus and wondering if they were little *monks*. When the teachers asked me what kind of counselor I envisioned myself being, I told them that I would be the informal kind, chatting away casually on a bench. I could never really see myself in a dress and heels behind a desk. I didn't like the idea of any power differential.

In Cleveland, I found something that changed my life for good: Emotions Anonymous (EA), a 12-step program. In my graduate program, I met Bill S., who became a good friend. He was in a 12-step program (AA) that had really worked for him. As with many things I had experienced on my road to sanity, I had conflicting thoughts and feelings about this new venture. I felt like maybe it could work for me, but I didn't want to be with people I considered "losers." Any group of people that identified together, based on a defect, scared me. I didn't want to pathologize myself.

Another challenge for me with a 12-step program was that I did not want to try a program based on God, and fail. God had all the power and the final say. If He couldn't heal me, nothing could. I didn't want to find out that I was hopeless. Bill tried to convince me to look into EA, but I dragged my feet.

I had been trying – unsuccessfully – to reignite friendships with dysfunctional people from my past. In Cleveland, my life was constantly triggered by the

CHAPTER 7

Goldberg family gatherings, where I felt inferior. I was overweight and had short, unattractive, dyed-blonde hair. I felt like an oddball and was still very depressed. Reaching my limit of suffering one day, I finally did act on the suicidal ideation I'd had for a decade. I took a bottle of Clonazepam – but fortunately, for my life – Bill called. He rushed me to the hospital.

I was overwhelmed. I don't think I really wanted to die. I remember lying in the emergency room after they pumped my stomach. My brother was to my right, crying (I didn't know he cared) and Bill was to my left. I was very drowsy. I somehow knew my life was about to change forever. No one forgets something like a suicide attempt.

What that experience taught me was that God did not want me to die. And I realized that I had to try Emotions Anonymous – it was the only thing left to try. What did I really have to lose? I almost lost my life. What was it worth?

So I tried EA, and it was a crucial transition on my road to healing. It turned out that in EA, I would be able to connect with people who had similar issues and experiences; people who could understand me. They might even be able to help me.

I needed to share my profound psychological problems and spiritual insights with like-minded people. EA would be a place where I could learn more about myself and share with others in an unthreatening environment. I wouldn't be dependent on one person anymore (thinking of Dr. B).

I began to spend time with the people in EA, who were very different from the super wealthy people I knew on the east side from my childhood. They were anything but "losers." They were honest. Everyone in EA struggled with issues, ranging from adjustment disorders to more serious diagnoses; and it was validating to know that I was not alone in my struggles. I was their equal, in that we were all raw and misunderstood. We talked about our problems without being judged, and we practiced the 12 steps. My world was finally filling up with real, three-dimensional people, because we were discussing feelings. It felt more like what I imagined the real world to be, because these people presented the content of their character and their emotions – rather than what they were wearing or driving. They talked about their weaknesses.

EA gave me so many gifts. Essentially, the most important breakthrough of EA for me was Step Three. Before Step Three is Step One – admitting you are

CHAPTER 7

powerless over your emotions. Step Two is coming to believe in a power greater than yourself. Step Three is turning your will and life over to the care of God. These steps started a process that strengthened my connection to, and guidance from, a Higher Power. It changed my life. Step Eleven, the presence of a Higher Power in our lives, is a continuation step that builds on Step Three. It is all about guidance. Step Three is a core part of how I live today (30 years later) and how I make all of my decisions.

The journey with my Higher Power has been amazing. It all started one day as I was sitting in my car. I felt my Higher Power (who I thought was Dr. B) contort my fingers in different ways. I felt that God was changing my behavioral conditioning.

Behaviors influence thoughts, and vice versa. I had spent my life mentally processing information, and there were always behaviors to match. When I broke this behavioral conditioning, I could change my thoughts – and therefore, my feelings. It was like the cognitive behavioral therapy I had done in college, only I was doing it to myself.

I began to hear a thought process in my head, guiding me when I didn't know where to go; when I was at an impasse. For example, in a driving situation, instead of turning my car to the right like I had always done, the thought would tell me to turn to the left. The thought in my head was like a silent voice. The EA program would often advise: "Since things have not worked out for you in the past, do the opposite of what you would normally do." The voice often told me to do something I thought was completely outrageous. But it was always right.

My Higher Power also told me what to say. When I had a question about how to behave, it gave me the answer. It is undeniably the best tool I have ever received. This guidance, over time, has become my intuition. Following my intuition *always* leads me to a good place. Sometimes, other members of EA ask how I have been so successful in living. I tell them that it was a blessing that my operating system in college fell apart, because – although devastating at the time – a new and much better system took its place.

Attending EA meetings three times a week facilitated the 12 steps in taking root. Now, I try to stay connected the best I can – usually one meeting a month for maintenance. I stay constantly linked with my Higher Power. The guidance I get from my intuition is always there – from little decisions to big ones. I have been using the connection since that day in the car, and I trust it implicitly after years of practice.

I say a prayer every morning, asking for "knowledge of God's will for me and the power to carry it out" to make sure I receive this guidance. And at the end of the day, I say, "Thank you." My Higher Power steers me into my own internal essence and spiritual self. Making the right decisions gives me confidence to be myself. I don't have to pretend to be someone else.

What surprises people – I think – is not only have I chosen to submit to this Higher Power, but also that I am actually *completely* dependent on this guidance. Without it, I have no way to make decisions. It is a gift to become dependent on God, who always knows better for my life than I do. God, through my intuition, has become my North Star. I feel that God gives me the ability to follow His advice or not. Although I love the guidance, I am also free. I can stray and make my own decisions (but they never turn out good)!

After Steps One, Two and Three – with the maintenance Step Eleven – comes Four and Five, which are steps about taking self-inventory and admitting those defects to another person. It is one thing to believe something, to communicate it with your Higher Power, but it takes telling another human being for it to feel real. This is actually Step Five in EA, to tell all three ("admitting to God, myself and another human being the exact nature of my wrongs"). It was easy for me to tell myself and God (still thinking of Dr. B); the challenge was telling another person. I was not very trusting. I only really trusted one person at the time, and that was Dr. B. But, I needed to share with other people. We are social beings living in a society that is based on consensual reality. It is hard to feel sane and included in a social group without sharing yourself with others.

Steps Six and Seven are the grace of the program. All they require are the readiness to admit defects, and the humility to ask to have them removed. You don't have to *do* anything. The wording of these steps imply that we cannot remove our defects on our own – if we could, we would – but that God will, if we are willing to get out of the way. It is impossible to remove a defect with the mind that created it. I have had many defects removed over the last 30 years. I have let go of a lot of bad habits. I feel so lucky. Character traits like jealousy, grandiosity, inferiority, and immobilizing sadness have disappeared. I tell people in my EA group to stick with the program, because it really works.

CHAPTER 7

Another gift that EA gave me was Step Eight: "Made a list of all persons we had harmed, and became willing to make amends to them all." The principle behind this step is discipline – taking accountability for one's actions. One result of my childhood – with parents like mine – was that I had problems with subsequent authority figures, rules and discipline. It did not feel safe in my childhood for me to submit to authority. Therefore, I often rebelled against rules, even stubbornly refusing to take care of myself. I resisted brushing my teeth or taking a shower, maybe because they were two of the few things I could control. I procrastinated and put things off, like doing my dirty dishes or my laundry. Emotions Anonymous taught me to turn off my "stinking thinking" and abide by the slogan, "Just Do It." But, more about the slogans in a bit!

The 8th and 9th Steps of making amends or restitution clear away the wreckage of the past and all of the guilt that comes with it. The program presumes that we all make mistakes – and will continue to make them – but we must assume responsibility for those errors in judgment. We must make amends in the form of an apology or a change in behavior. These steps gave me a way to feel fully human, although not perfect; and a way to make up for past mistakes and improve my behavior. The 10th step allows for the continuation of the process of self-reflection. The 11th step, as I mentioned earlier, is the continuation of Steps One, Two and Three.

A huge part of the 12-step program is helping others, or service. This is, in fact, Step Twelve. Service to others is one of the important ways that I continue to stay well. I try to help out when I see a need – whether it is to stay on the phone a little longer with someone, or to help clean up after a party.

Service includes sponsoring other people within the EA program. Once I finished going through the 12 steps with my own sponsor, I sponsored other people. That was enormously helpful, not just to the other person (the sponsee), but to me too. They say that what you teach, you really need to learn. I benefited greatly from hearing my sponsees' problems. I always found something I could relate to. Their problems always mirrored my own, and I could listen to my own advice.

Twelve-step programs have many helpful slogans. Here are two slogans that continually help me: "Easy Does It" and "First Things First." There are also many motivating promises of how life will improve after following the steps, such as "you will seek to understand, rather than being understood" and "you will intuitively know how to handle situations that used to baffle you." These simple sayings instilled hope in me and came true!

Another helpful trope in EA is: "HALT: Hungry, Angry, Lonely, Tired." It reminds me that most problems I experience are the result of one or more of those conditions. A lot of what we experience when we suffer from a mental illness can be sorted out by: food, sleep, talking and connection. This is true for all humans. Being hungry, angry, lonely or tired can make us feel *crazy*. I learned that, just because I was feeling uncomfortable or out-of-sorts, it did not mean I was crazy. Habitually, I would use my intuition to figure out if I was suffering from one of the states I just mentioned, and then I would take the necessary action to fix the situation. If it was food I needed, I ate. If I was angry, I processed the anger internally or took action. If I was lonely, I called a friend. If I was tired, I slept. And then, I always felt better.

Sleep also gave the added benefit of a break in my mind chatter, and allowed guidance by my Higher Power in dreams! I have solved a lot of problems that way. Our mind can be a dangerous place, and it is important to align it with our higher self or Higher Power. Sometimes, it is important just to turn it off.

It can also be important to turn off one's mouth! One lesson that really made sense, and stuck with me, is that we are given two ears and one mouth – to listen twice as much as we talk! Between what was modeled for me in childhood and my natural tendencies, I was self-centered and talked a lot. When I learned to really listen, instead of rehearsing in my mind what I was going to say, it was amazing how much I learned. It was surprising to realize that maybe no response was even required. Humility is an ongoing lesson.

EA showed me that in a healthy environment, people care and help one another; they share freely and support each other, rather than hide their good ideas. EA was the opposite of my childhood's competitive environment. I was continuing to learn and creating a world in which I wanted to live, rather than a world that was selfish and even cutthroat. Instead of fighting over resources, we could have a bigger pie.

More practically, in EA, I learned about the common problems that patients have with the mental health system. Often, because of their illnesses, they are insecure about their opinions and they let the mental health clinicians do too much directing. While the experts may have more information, there's also a time to trust your gut when a medication or therapist is not working for you. I counseled people about how to stick up for themselves.

We always said that EA means Equal Adults. It was helpful not to have any so-called experts or professional psychotherapists in the room. That released me from the embarrassment of disclosing any weaknesses. Due to a power differential in psychotherapy, which made me feel inferior, I always felt judged and discouraged from sharing there. But EA was a place that allowed me to grow and recover, and I will forever be grateful that I found it – or that it found me.

CHAPTER 8
MARRIED WITH CHILDREN

1999

Emotions Anonymous helped me enormously. I had friends who I could call and with whom I could get together. I also had meaningful relationships with my stepbrother Dan and his wife, Carrie. My mom remarried when I was in college; Dan was my roommate for a while.

I had been in EA for at least a year and I felt like a fledgling deer, just starting to stand on my own feet. But I was *standing*. That is key here, because I would never have been able to start dating anyone if I wasn't.

It was New Year's Eve 1998, turning into 1999. Dan and Carrie had invited me – along with other friends – to a party. I brought a date because I didn't know that it was supposed to be a blind date. But, I was sitting at the end of the table when I saw Kurt burning a pizza box. I thought he was cute. Kurt ended up talking to my date most of the night, because I drank too much. Then, Kurt called me a couple of days later and asked me out! The evening worked out as planned, and Kurt and I started dating.

I was so excited. I still had a long way to go in my recovery, but he *liked* me. My other date went by the wayside. Kurt and I went to a fancy restaurant to dance for our first date. I was smitten; I thought he was adorable, and I waited anxiously for his call for the second date.

He was not flashy like a Goldberg, which I liked. He wore similar khaki pants and polo shirts every day. He did not care about impressing anyone. He was smart and had money, and a good job. He had earned a bachelor's degree from Michigan, along with a plethora of graduate degrees, including a JD from Columbia and an MBA from NYU. Although he was super smart, he was imperfect, which made me feel comfortable. He was messy and disorganized – and human! On one of our first dates, I brought my truck to help him move out of his apartment. He brought out full drawers

CHAPTER 8

of disorganized clutter to move to the new house. I laughed to myself. We were the same!

Most importantly, when I spoke to Kurt, I felt like my ideas made sense. I wasn't given the quizzical looks I was always given by the Goldbergs when I talked. Honesty wasn't a threat to him. I was thrilled that someone so successful and nice liked me! I fell head over heels in love with him!

We got engaged six months later. We went to Capri to celebrate and we had a deep conversation there. I realized I could even help him! I remember explaining that the key to good conversations was *disclosure*. (I had learned a lot about that topic in therapy.) He acted like I had given him the holy grail. In turn, I felt like he gave me the holy grail throughout our marriage, every time he protected me from the overwhelming influence of the outside world.

He supported me through depressive and manic episodes. One manic episode occurred in Northern California where we took our two children. I was so manic that I wasn't able to control the toddlers from pooping on the floor in the hotel room. Kurt did not judge; he helped me get through it and didn't ever complain.

Not everyone would have stuck around like Kurt did. I don't know if I would be where I am without him.

If I had been healthier, I would have paid attention to two major red flags, however. First, Kurt had a temper. I saw an example early on in our dating life, and it scared me. He got really mad about something and threw a pillow across the room. This kind of temper, maybe minor to someone else, was not good for me. It triggered a memory of the rage I had seen in my parents. But he said it was "just a pillow."

Kurt and I were married in July of 2000. Kurt wanted to please my mother by letting her pay for the wedding. Although I had come a long way, I was still not able to stand up for myself. The wedding became a very unpleasant experience for me – my mother was very controlling, and she seemed unaware that it was *my* wedding. She did everything, from picking out the flowers to creating the guest list. She ended up inviting about 100 extra people without telling me; I didn't recognize most of the people at my wedding. At the food tasting, she, and my brother and his wife, ate away, hardly consulting me about what I thought about the food.

The other red flag from Kurt that I ignored happened on our wedding day. I was all dressed up and

CHAPTER 8

excited, with tears of joy. I teared up when I saw Kurt for the first time in his suit. Instead of sharing in my excitement, he told me to "calm down." My enthusiasm felt squelched. Kurt and I handle emotions differently.

But I was in love with Kurt, and he was my way back into society. I married him and became a member of the mainstream. I left my reclusive life in my apartment and moved into his house in a middle-class neighborhood. I was a regular person! I started to create a personality that could interact adequately in public. Up until that time, I had been part of two extremes – either the Goldbergs, or with people who were struggling with mental health. Now, I was in the middle. Even more important, my married life was not an *as-if personality*. It felt honest, even if there were still some fake remnants left to be burned.

Kurt wanted to be a young father and have children right away, which surprised me. I was hoping to have some time for just the two of us to adjust to married life. But I was insecure, and I thought Kurt knew best. I felt happy and deferred to his judgment on most everything. Plus, I was very excited to have children. We were surprised when we found out we were having twins!

The boys were born blue. The doctor had to vacuum Jacob out about two hours after Sam came out. The doctor said there was nothing to worry about. Even though the babies did not have to spend time in the neonatal intensive care unit, I was worried. Weren't babies supposed to cry when they came out?

Other worries surfaced at their 18-month-old checkup when they failed to reach certain milestones, mostly in terms of speech. Kurt and I felt very connected to our loving sons, but my mother sent us an article about the Cleveland Clinic School for Autism. She had seen many babies, children and grandchildren, and she thought something was wrong with our boys.

We started banging pots and pans behind them, as the books suggested, to test for autism. The boys did not turn around. The pediatrician and neurologist said not to worry, it was just speech delay. Even the autism specialist said that if it was autism, it appeared mild. But she recommended that they both go to a special school. We enrolled them at 2 ½ years old.

Both boys ended up being severely autistic. They have very few word approximations, need 24-hour care, and are not fully potty-trained at age 22.

I felt like the Goldbergs had finally beaten me. I had *inferior*, special-needs children. I had lost the status war.

CHAPTER 8

I was embarrassed to bring my boys to family events. I would spend hours dressing them up in uncomfortable, expensive clothes just so they would fit in. They were unable to speak or play with any of the other children. Nobody ever paid attention to them anyway.

When my mother looked at my boys, she cried. She saw their condition as a tragedy. She said visiting them made her too sad. She would invite us over to her house, but make no accommodations for them. She would throw a fit when chocolate milk was spilled. Even so, she insisted on being called "Mima," which I saw as too similar to "mommy," a name I felt *I* deserved. I changed her name to "Gammy." She was not happy about it.

It was Goldberg protocol for parents to use the money that my grandfather made to provide for schooling for the grandkids. My mother provided financially for Jake and Sam's schooling, which I really appreciated. They went to the Cleveland Clinic School for Autism, which was one of the best in the country (just like the article had stated). They were enrolled in a disciplined Applied Behavior Analysis (ABA) curriculum. We investigated other modalities, but ABA was considered the premier data-driven and proven therapy.

Everything was incredibly expensive. The Cleveland Clinic School for Autism started at $72,000 per year, and increased over the years. Jacob went there until the age of 22. Sam switched to an equally expensive and wonderful school, KidsLink, when he was kicked out of the Cleveland Clinic due to violent behavior at age 12 (Sam had been diagnosed with bipolar disorder). For tutors to help at home, it cost us $25 per hour, which eventually inflated to $30 per hour. When I brought my mother to an attorney to see if she would provide any future assurance for their financial well-being (she has millions of dollars), she offered nothing. She could have put my mind at ease if she had wanted to, but she didn't. Thankfully, Kurt made a good living, and has been able to provide for the boys.

Aside from the amount of arduous work that caring for the boys' autism entailed, as mania expanded my *inner* universe, the boys' autism has expanded my *outer* universe. The universe is really *that* big – with all kinds of people and all kinds of perspectives. I was finally becoming comfortable with diversity: special needs, people of different ethnicities, and a plethora of different viewpoints. Living with diversity was unlike the homogeneity of my upbringing.

The boys taught me to think outside of the *linear box* of the world. They don't operate on a chronological timeline. They are easily distracted and in the moment. I needed to *feel* their feelings with them, instead of depending on logical speech, which they did not have. I paid attention to their needs through body language and associative cues. There was no verbal conversation, but there was always dialogue. We love each other. They developed my patience and tolerance. Their needs demanded a lot of self-sacrifice and service. Service is always self-expanding.

The Goldberg way of perfection was blown to bits, and so was my *as-if personality*. Once I became comfortable with the boys' diagnosis, it lifted me out of the world of status. The two-dimensional world was no longer. One thing for sure, the boys didn't have any status. They were free of societal trappings. They were loving, pure, and free of agenda. What you saw was what you got. I could trust them. They offered me a world of love and acceptance for who I was *inside*. All they wanted from me was love. Because of my history, I am still very wary of human beings. But it is a joy just existing in the present with my boys. They have the same loving presence that I experience with my dogs – such a beautiful thing. Jake and Sam are two of my favorite people.

My illness was placed on the back burner; the needs of my sons mandated that I become more *other-centered*. I no longer felt impaired; it was a relief to not be the "sick one."

At the time Samuel and Jacob were born, the autistic birth rate skyrocketed. There are now many people on the autism spectrum in the population. In my experience, after interacting with Samuel and Jacob for 22 years, I see they are on a completely different wavelength from the neurotypical (which is the fancy word for normal). They think differently, which can be demonstrated by what they are able and unable to do. They can be content doing the same thing for hours – like time is standing still.

On the other hand, they can be constantly in motion. They are not concerned about what people think of them. They see little details, joy in simple things; and they have great senses of humor. In terms of their physical senses, their hearing is augmented and they are sensitive to itchy clothing. They do not plan, and do not seem to be aware of time.

Their simplicity challenges me to expand my awareness, which can feel like ushering in another dimension. Maybe a fourth one! I wonder if they operate more on the level of quantum physics, which postulates that time does not exist. I don't notice much of a reaction from them when I come back from being gone a long time. I think the present is a big, long *now* for them. Instead of marginalizing them as sick, I welcome them – as I welcome mania – as perspectives to be respected. They notice things we do not. They hear things we do not. They feel things we do not.

In 2004, two years after Samuel and Jacob were born, we had a daughter, Emma. She is a firecracker and is neurotypical; not autistic. Because we were overwhelmed with the boys, she basically raised herself. Out of necessity (or because of our own natural parenting styles and her independent nature), Kurt and I gave her a very long leash. We hardly ever corrected her. My aunt told me to refrain from telling Emma how smart she was, lest she would rule the roost. But that was not our style. While we didn't overinflate her, we gave her a voice.

Kurt and I co-parented well for a while, but his ability to squelch my enthusiasm – while good when I had a manic episode – became depressing and felt invalidating after I outgrew my illness in my 40s.

One of the clinicians at the National Institute of Mental Health had told my father that once the bipolar was taken care of, the borderline would go away. It did. Bipolar is a medical condition that can be managed by medication, and it fades with age. The borderline aspects of my personality went away as my moods stabilized. Over time, I was able to have more object constancy and relationship interdependence.

I became more independent, and as I recovered, Kurt and I now fought over a lot of things: staff for our boys, whether or not to get pets, and where he was putting his attention. Although I still loved him, I realized we were not the best fit anymore. In the beginning, his stoicism was a calming strength for me, but it had come to feel like a lack of emotional support.

The final straw was Belize. Kurt and I were worried that we would not be able to provide for the boys long-term, so we wanted to see if living in Belize, a third-world country, would be a more affordable option. By the time we got there, we knew we were financially secure with impending state aid; but I had always wanted beachfront property, and I loved it in Belize. Kurt and I had been searching for beachfront property for years on different vacations. Here, it was affordable. I could buy a condo with the cash in my bank account! It felt like home.

I realize now that if our marriage had been in a better place at the time, I probably wouldn't have bought a house in Belize, since Kurt didn't want to spend a lot of time there. But by then, we were sleeping in different bedrooms, and hardly sharing information with each other – let alone feelings. I think I really wanted a house in Belize so I could have something to look forward to – a place to have some happiness.

There were a few things that happened around the time of the Belize purchase that eventually led to our demise. As we were buying the house in Belize, Kurt spent almost two full days texting my brother. I'm not sure why Kurt involved my brother, except that he often put my family before me. Maybe it was because of the Goldberg money. I have always felt that Kurt was preoccupied with the children's inheritance. I'm sure it was obvious to Kurt that I was putting the Belize house before him.

Kurt didn't confront me personally about his concerns. But involving my brother was upsetting to me. I did not like how my brother tried to control me and take charge of my life. Since my time at Menninger decades prior, he has tried to kidnap me from treatment (pulling me into his car at Menninger), push me prematurely to get a divorce, and take over my financial affairs. He was never supportive of my mental health treatment.

My brother and Kurt decided that Kurt should call my psychiatrist and tell her I needed a mental health check. Kurt never gave me a heads-up; I was blindsided when my psychiatrist called me. It was a sign for me that our communication and trust in each other was broken. I felt betrayed.

The psychiatrist gave me a clean bill of health, and the experience gave me the confidence I needed to end our marriage. I realized we were no longer a team. Ironically, Dr. B had already told me to get divorced months earlier when I described my marriage to him. I divorced Kurt.

I wouldn't have been able to divorce Kurt if I hadn't done all the preparatory work I had done in Emotions

CHAPTER 8

Anonymous and in therapy – and certainly not as quickly without Dr. B's mandate. It takes courage to break out of a role played for so long, especially with an *as-if personality* disorder. Kurt had always made me feel safe. I had struggled mentally for much of our marriage; for a long time, I felt comfortable playing the role of a person who needed guidance.

Divorce forced me to let go of my role as a wife and my codependency on Kurt. Wikipedia describes codependency as an "imbalanced relationship where one person enables another's self-destructive behavior." In our case, I deferred taking responsibility, and I let Kurt make all the decisions. It took a lot of courage to stand naked in the world without Kurt's protection. Entering into a new, unknown world where I needed to stand on my own two feet was a challenge. But, when I made the move (even applying to Starbucks to obtain insurance and a paycheck because I didn't know if I would have enough money), I knew intuitively that it was the path I needed to follow.

Not long after the divorce, things with Emma became tough. While the respect we gave her had reaped great rewards, it was also challenging for her and me. She is very outspoken, and during her teenage years, she became angry with me. I was triggered by her anger, as it reminded me of my mother's rage. We fought a lot; I thought it best for her – and for me – that she go live with her father. It was a devastating time for me, as I really missed her.

Our separation was also hard because I felt like I had failed as a mother. The last thing I ever wanted was to follow in my mother's footsteps. However, the time apart proved invaluable for me. I realized that I had actually overcompensated and had become codependent with Emma. I hung onto every word Emma said, trying to fix everything, which she hated. I had to learn how to adjust expectations – pulling back, letting my daughter be herself, and finding myself in the process.

It seemed to work out well for her as well. She became a speaker at her high school graduation, leader on the debate team, and went to Stanford. We are quite proud of her. I learned the hard way. A relationship with a child can be a very good way of mirroring our own behavior back to us.

Emma played a huge role in my individuation process and the shedding of my *as-if personality*. There was a children's book called *Dorothy Must Die*, by Danielle Paige, that I once noticed on Emma's bookshelf. While

CHAPTER 8

I never read the book – or knew what it was about – when I saw the title, my first thought was that Emma was going to kill me. I didn't understand it at the time, but that was exactly what happened. My *as-if personality* was the main character (Dorothy), and it had to die. Emma's criticisms of me, and rejection of me after she left to live with her dad, caused my *as-if personality* to die. I cried and suffered for about three years, mourning the death of the personality I had lived with for 50 years.

At the same time in my life, I learned how intertwined my *as-if personality* was with codependency. I realized how codependent I was acting in the rest of my life. I was constantly putting other people's needs ahead of my own with people-pleasing behavior. I had learned from my parents that other people's feelings were more important than mine. I worried about making other people feel safe. That's how I operated in the world.

In my mid-50s, I learned a very important lesson from a highly codependent neighbor in Florida. She changed her tune overnight – from being in dire straits and having me very worried about her, to having nothing wrong in her life the next day. I realized my emotional commitment was being played. I let go of that relationship, which had been challenging. I finally felt free to find people with whom I could be honest and independent – and they could be the same with me.

Codependency began and ended with my father. He was the origin, and the last piece that I finally released. As a child, he called me his "partner" and his "little mother." The nature of his dependency was driven home by my grandmother, his mother, who told me on her deathbed that he was helpless. I felt like I had to take care of him, which I did until I was 54.

Throughout my teens, 20s, 30s, and 40s, my dad called me roughly five to 10 times a day, a practice he started when he moved to Florida when I was 15. I begged him for decades to stop; he refused. I don't think he could even *hear* what I was saying, because he certainly didn't change his behavior. I think the ADD played a large part.

Later in life, once I was in a relationship that met my emotional needs, I was able to let go of the toxic relationship I had with my father. I finally understood how codependency had been the currency in most of my relationships. I finally blocked my dad on my phone so I couldn't receive anymore calls and texts.

Codependency, as a generational habit, is very hard to break. I believe it is the most prevalent addiction, maybe next to food, because we can't stay away from either people or food. I stopped the cycle.

Although I was not the parent I had hoped to be, I was successful in achieving my goal that Emma be her own person psychologically. She is neither codependent or a pretender. I am ecstatic about this.

Today, Kurt is the most wonderful ex-husband I could ask for. He manages the boys for me while I live out of state. Neither of us have ever wanted to put them in an institution. We staff them out of our homes and they go back and forth. Kurt is generous with his wealth.

He is a wonderful father to Emma, as he has always been. We agree that continuing to give our successful daughter a long leash is best. We are both happier. Even Emma says so. Kurt and I spent 19 years together, and he was and is a large part of my life. He is a person of immense generosity and integrity.

CHAPTER 9
UNBELIZEABLE

2015 - 2020

The house we were to buy together on Ambergris Caye in San Pedro, Belize, turned out to be only for me. I took the time to make that house a home where I could bring my most treasured friends. I flowered and flourished when I was in Belize. It turned out to be the most climactic and adventurous time of my life. I felt a strong sense of self, taking such a huge risk. I went four times a year; I was alone in a foreign country, far away from my family, in an environment that was totally different from the United States. It was just my speed. I loved the way they did things there. Everyone drove around in golf carts and bought vegetables from stands on the side of the road. It was the definition of a simple life.

Aside from getting my coveted beach property, Belize gave me the courage I don't think I could have learned any other way. It was a foreign country; it was a risky move; and it catapulted everyone around me into action, showing their true colors. People in my life had strong reactions.

No one knew what Stacy was doing! I was breaking the family protocol by buying a vacation home so early in life, and in a *foreign* country! The Goldberg way was threatened, and the gaslighting started. I got a million confusing comments meant to deter me from buying. "It's too far." "There's too much crime." "What will you do for medical assistance?"

My brother, Steve, tried to sabotage the sale. He told me that if I bought the property, I would lose all family support. I thought I saw him driving around my home in Cleveland in his Range Rover, trying to lay eyes on me in order to *prove* I was crazy. He never did see me or speak to me, but he told Kurt to "cut off the money." I think Kurt was taken aback by that, and he said it wasn't his money anyway.

Who knows what motivations my brother had? I used to rationalize his behavior as his way of taking care of me, until I realized that when I really needed him in my life, he was never there. When I was extremely depressed and lonely, and we were living in the same apartment complex, he never visited me. And the same thing had occurred years earlier, when we lived one street away from each other.

I once asked him for budgeting help when my finances were a mess. When he said he would help, I took all of my bills to his apartment, and he spent the whole time flirting with his girlfriend. His constant talk about protecting me – about serving as what he called my *backstop* – was just hot air. Kurt might have been controlling (even though I could excuse him for wanting to keep the marriage together), but my brother was downright power-hungry. As I said earlier, he had become my mother's partner in crime at a very early age, which meant that he was not concerned with my best interests. He was concerned with hers. My brother is now out of my life.

Belize gave me the discernment I needed. It helped me separate the wheat from the chaff in my life. It helped me sever my relationship with my family, starting with my brother. My mother also stood on the sidelines, and did not support me.

A big part of getting rid of my *as-if personality* was discerning who to hang out with – deciding who freed me and who reinforced the fake personality.

If I felt I was trying to fit in, I knew I was being fake. Starting with Belize, I became more forceful in eradicating unhealthy people from my life. People who contributed to my sense of feeling false, in any way, had to go. Belize was the culmination of truly feeling myself – my true self, the self I had been working so hard for so many years to find. Belize became the defining moment of my life.

Separating from my family was like escaping a cult. I was finally seeing the clues and piecing the pieces together. "Goldberg paternalism" was toxic for me. I was sick of people always saying they were "taking care" of me. People who spoke cryptically and manipulatively were not to be trusted. I was now not bound to the homeland of my upbringing. I was able to set down new roots in a totally different land. With my faith in my Higher Power, there was no stopping me. I was becoming my own person. I was developing my long-sought-after personal agency. I now wanted someone who would support and enable the separation from my family.

CHAPTER 10

A SOULMATE MAKES LIFE COME TO LIFE

2018 - Forever

Sometimes, you have to walk even when you know there isn't a path just yet. It appears to meet your feet as you move. The path continues to form with each risk you take, until you finally get where you need to go. Robert was my path.

We met on a dating site. He looked different from anyone I had ever known from the east side. He was from the west side of Cleveland, where they dressed differently, acted differently, and even spoke differently! They didn't wear clothes from Kilgore Trout, which was the most expensive and frequented clothing shop for men on the east side. I purposely picked him out from an array of potential suitors because he was from the west side. He wouldn't know, or be influenced by, my family, I thought. Both thoughts turned out to be true.

On our third date, I explained the difficulties I had with my family, and Robert said, "They are not good for you. You would be better off without them." He gave me the confidence and financial support I needed to finally separate from them.

This was the relationship where I could *come out*, and act and speak with complete honesty. I revealed some of the strange things about me; I even told him I thought I was Jesus. His response, laughingly, was, "Oh! I get to have sex with Jesus!" He just made everything OK. We enjoyed doing the same things. To this day, I am perfectly content on this plateau with him, just enjoying our relationship. I want for nothing.

I loved his kids immediately. I felt comforted and listened to by them. They accepted me exactly as I am. I didn't feel the need to dress a certain way around them. Unlike my Goldberg family, they don't correct me when I speak. I am able to get out full sentences. There is no judgment or argument or trying to change my mind. I feel supported in expressing my opinions.

I never knew why it was so difficult for me to speak while growing up in the Goldberg family. But it became obvious to me once I became an adult: I asked too many questions. I pointed out things that they wanted hidden; I challenged the status quo; I asked questions about my trust fund and the family business. Kurt and I even hired a lawyer to press for information about my money when we were concerned about how we were going to pay for the boys. My relatives were defensive. I'm sure they tried to pigeonhole me as unstable or crazy – the proof, of course, was that I had been in a mental hospital.

With Robert's kids, I felt something I never would have thought I could feel – acceptance. I also was able to feel love for someone else's kids; love like they were my own kids. This feeling of acceptance was shared by all of the people I met on the west side. They were normal people! By normal, I mean, they had no attitude of superiority and didn't try to hide their imperfections. I'm not saying everybody was perfect or had perfect lives, but they were open. Their humility helped me accept my humanity, flaws and all. I met people who meant what they said, did what they said they would do, and didn't pretend. They had weaknesses – but they were genuine!

Robert and I were engaged a year after we met, and married after five years. He became the partner I had always needed and wanted. Kurt helped me get halfway there. Robert completed the way. Robert completes *me*. He is my soulmate.

With Robert, I finally solved my sexual issues. I am comfortable with (even love!) my body for the first time in my life. We have a full, healthy sexual life. We are so comfortable with each other that all of my sexual hangups and fears went away.

He accepted my boys – the poopy diapers, and even my one son's violence. Sam breaks everything in the house and Robert fixes it! I thought I was dreaming, I was so lucky! I thought I would never find anyone who would accept me with my adult, autistic twin boys.

My mother and brother rejected Robert outright. My mother said she would never date anyone from the west side, and for months wouldn't agree to meet him. She didn't invite him to Rosh Hashanah. The first time that Robert and my brother met, my brother mocked him and treated him condescendingly.

I was happy for the first time in my life, after all my suffering, and my mother and brother were trying to take away my happiness. They behaved in a way that securely closed the door on my relationships with them. Having a hero show up who was subsequently rejected by my family told me everything I needed to know.

CHAPTER 10

My relationship with my birth family was based on image. It was patronizing, posing, and dominating. In my new life, I realized that real relationships are based on honesty, openness, disclosure and feelings. But as I was beginning a new life on the west side, I began to mourn my old one on the east side. The constant shedding of my *as-if personality* was both a happy revelation and a deep sadness. There was now hope for me; but I was reminded that I had to let go of the first 50 years of my life, including relationships that had meant so much at one time. It was like experiencing death on a mass scale.

Looking back, it astounds me that I survived 50 years living without real intimacy. It amazes me that I had a feeling of falsehood for so long; that it took 50 years of my life to become truly honest. There were hundreds of layers of lies to work through. I'm also surprised I was able to survive the loneliness and didn't go completely insane. My mind was all over the place for so long, obsessing almost constantly.

I rekindled a friendship with a childhood friend, Sara, that confirmed the authenticity I had in my relationship with Robert. We got to know each other in an entirely new, intimate way. She told me, ironically (and hysterically, to me!) that she had always idolized me as a child. To her, I had it all together! It was flattering – but boy, I realized that our new, more authentic connection was more important than trying to impress her!

With my new family, I felt rewarded, just like I had felt rewarded with the experience of mania. I felt God sent me another sign that I was on the right track, through the gift of a soulmate for the second half of my life. We met more people who fit into our lifestyle when we moved to Florida.

During the COVID pandemic, I received an ad on my social media for a beachfront hotel room for $500 for a week! In Englewood, Florida. (Where? Never heard of it.)

At first impression after traveling there, I didn't like it. It didn't seem fancy enough. It seemed like it was tacky – for poor people. A Goldberg would never visit there! By the end of the week, I wanted to buy a place there.

The area was full of wildlife. It wasn't dead like the east coast of Florida, where I had lived 30 years ago. Robert was catching one fish after another, just

CHAPTER 10

standing on the beach with his line in the ocean! I could easily trade status for this natural world.

After much discussion, including the fact that my boys couldn't visit me in Belize (too far), and that I wanted a place to retire in warmth (as did Robert), I became convinced that it was now time to sell my place in Belize and move to this area in Florida.

Before I knew it, I was living in Placida, right next to Englewood, for three weeks a month. I went home to Cleveland for one week a month to see my boys. Ironically, Florida was where Dr. B had told me I would eventually live. From Dr. B's description, I imagined Florida as a place where things would make sense. I had presumed Dr. B knew my future and would always be right. He was.

I tried one more time with my mother when I moved to Florida, and I invited her to come visit. She said, "Yeah, right," sarcastically. I didn't fully realize it at the time, but she was actually telling me she would never visit. It was like I had lost my mother. I was no longer doing things her way and I had stopped pretending, so she had no need for me anymore. I was devastated as the truth finally stared me in the face – she never really loved me. Love is wanting someone else's happiness.

I was now on my own, forced to try my hand at *living real* with my new neighbors in Placida, Florida. I began going to dinner parties and boating trips and I met people. I still had to sift through people, but after meeting a few couples who actually listened and let me speak, I knew what I was looking for and what I needed. They were not controlling or codependent. They heard me and validated my opinions. One friend from Florida actually said, "How could your mother not like you? You are so nice!"

I practiced focusing on what people were actually saying, not being distracted by externality – clothes or physical appearance. I had to get used to people looking different than people from the east side of Cleveland did. It became about *inner* connection. It was about trust. It was scary speaking from the heart – the center of myself – and not saying what I thought everybody wanted to hear. With practice, it became easier. I realized I can say anything, as long as I watch my manners. There are no rules. We are all just trying to figure it out together.

Now I have emotions that have come alive and that I can feel when I talk to people. I look into their eyes, and I see and feel a whole, diverse, huge world in their soul. I don't stereotype. If I like a person, I listen to what they are saying, and if I *feel* like they're being genuine, I move forward with them. I trust my intuition. If those boxes get checked off, I feel a response well up in me that I know to be true. I can act accordingly. Step 11 holds true!

Now I have responses that are authentic and not preplanned, not coined phrases. Now I find myself just talking, surprising myself, creating! I don't actually know what I am going to share! What is God guiding me to share? I want to connect. I see the other person as a human, just like me. I finally feel I know what it is like to be human, because I am getting comfortable with living life in the three dimensions. I see a fellow human before me who – I presume – has a plethora of feelings just like me; and I feel confident that if I talk authentically, they will be able to understand me.

I no longer have patience for anyone who displays themself in a superficial way. Not only does it feel empty, but it also feels abusive and induces post-traumatic stress in me. Sometimes, I will get a feeling when someone talks to me, or when I see a familiar "Goldberg mannerism" (like over-smiling or not sharing anything personal over a long period of time), and I know that he or she is not a person who would be good for me. Or sometimes, the other person shares too much too early, and that can be a red flag for codependency.

I try to stay away from people who are struggling and don't want to change. If I can help, I love to try to do that, but the person has to be willing. If the person is not willing, guidance from Emotions Anonymous says to move on to the next person who might really need my help and won't waste my time. My life is about service. I still try to offer help at EA meetings, and I volunteer as a hospice pet therapist.

My aunt tried to contact me at the end of her life; but sadly, I knew that any interaction would be toxic. She was one of those people who always needed to be perfect. It was a difficult relationship to sever, because she truly helped me when she took me to the hospital. But, perfectionism is a definite red flag!

Now I try to only be around equal human beings who find themselves here on this planet with nothing to prove or brag about – just people who enjoy connecting. The world I have now has replaced a world based on status, and a childhood where I felt I could only talk to people who were wealthy, good-looking and thin. I am happy that there is no "superior" or "inferior," because it is very hard to have relationships with people when you feel better or worse than them. The greatest gift I have received from living in a three-dimensional reality is that I have so many more people to talk to!

FINISH

This is my story so far. I overcame an *as-if personality*, which was compromised with a mood disorder. Today, I have a happy, full and healthy life. It took decades of practice to create a life that I wanted to live. I exhausted the traditional methods of psychotherapy and medication, and found supplemental solutions. With an *as-if personality*, I had to reject what I learned in childhood, and intellectualize a new identity, because I couldn't trust my feelings for a long time. I studied human nature whenever I could – in people, in books, magazines, television and movies. Through trial and error, and with good people who listened to my thoughts and ideas, I realized I could try many ways of living. It gave me the courage to let go of a 50-year past filled with people, relatives and friends. Only a few people made it through to the other side.

The good news, for me, was that I crafted my life from scratch, based on well-thought-out, intuitive decisions. I built my existence from the ground up. The result is a strong, unshakable foundation. Now, I find myself in a life tailor-made for me. I sometimes annoy people, because I have such little tolerance for anything that seems inauthentic. Because of the pretense in my childhood, I am allergic to anything or anyone false; I become confused and disoriented. After years of accruing self-confidence, if things start to feel confusing, I am now better at questioning the outer circumstance rather than myself. I'm really good at handling almost anything or anyone who is being real.

For the first time in my life, in my 50s, I understand what is going on around me. I can understand the news, current events, and why somebody is acting a certain way. I have a basic understanding of what it is like to be human. Although we are all different, we have basic things in common.

It has helped to find love and a new family. I don't know if self-acceptance can arrive without validation from someone else. I hope that anyone who reads this – who may be suffering from an *as-if personality* or any other personality disorder – can find someone who accepts and helps them. It can be professional (or nonprofessional) help – whatever guides one to one's own intuition.

CHAPTER 10

For me, it took belief in a Higher Power to have faith in the capacity for change. Although I was gifted with courage and resilience, I was unable to do it by myself. Emotions Anonymous gave me a design for living and a framework for the perpetual guidance that I believe comes from God. (For anyone interested, please contact emotionsanonymous.org.)

A whole new world opened up to me in mania, a world that made sense and was not dark and useless. Although I cannot see its intensity all the time, the manic perspective gives me the motivation to keep going. It was my best friend, up and down through depressive and manic episodes, until I finally felt stable in the world. The manic viewpoint is always in the back of my mind. Although I have dark days, I feel like I have reached enlightenment because I am filled with love for other people and myself. What kept me suffering all of those years was a feeling of alienation from the rest of society and an existential loneliness.

I will never forget all the persistent, constant anger I felt at everyone – and at myself – for 50 years. It came from childhood wounding, and could only be healed through a re-mothering. Healing must include trusting new people when you have been hurt in your childhood. That takes courage, because everything in your body will tell you to stay guarded – lest you feel the pain you felt before.

My guard was my *as-if personality*. Unfortunately, I see movements, such as social media and fashion magazines, in our society that seem to promote pretense. I sometimes wonder if we're living in a somewhat *as-if world*. I am concerned that there are elements of today's culture that seduce people to live in two dimensions, posing and posturing. That's not where the gold resides. The gold may not reside in a family name that you thought you could trust at one time – it resides on the *inside*, in the three dimensions. When you open your inside – faults and all – to someone else's inside, the magic happens.

Today, I listen to Christian radio stations and read the Bible, not because I consider myself a Christian, but because I consider myself to be a form of Jesus Christ. I died and rose from the dead. Maybe we are all Jesus Christ. He's just a model for us to follow. He was an example of a sacrificial lamb who benefited others. As we change, we change others. Because of my struggles, many transformations occurred in my life and the lives around me. I have turned my life over to the will and power of God. I don't know who the living historical

CHAPTER 10

Jesus Christ is from the Bible, but I know I identify with him.

Today I am grounded in a new way. Maybe I just can't fathom existing as the *Stacy* of my childhood. Maybe I just need a larger spiritual context to view and validate myself. My struggles seem larger than life to me. Because I had a caregiver I perceived to be evil, my life became a lifelong struggle of deciphering good versus evil. It caused me to become very philosophical and morally consumed. It demanded the spiritual plane. The pinprick scope of my upbringing just couldn't provide a foundation for the full existence of Stacy. Maybe Jesus has led me to a larger definition of who Stacy can be.

I shy away from giving advice, because I am not an expert on your life like you are. However, I recommend you find what works for *you*. Other people can only tell you what they read in books, study in school, or know from their own lives. Be cautious about letting anyone tell you how to think about your illness. You got yourself here, now you have to get yourself back.

After all, I found meaning in loose objects I found on the street. Other people may not understand that, but it worked for me. I searched for meaning in everything that happened to me, because if I was going to get well, I had to accept my illness and all its manifestations and aberrations. I had to love myself; all of myself. So find what works for you. It may take a few tries, and may involve some strange things, but it will be worth it.

I was mandated by my Higher Power (who I suspect to be Dr. B) to write this book. I was worried about slandering people. That is not my intent. This is about telling *my* truth and feeling whole. There is something about the process of writing and seeing my life in black and white that manifests my existence. Writing the music that I hear in my soul into this book gives me a *feeling* of validity. I want to stay in the three-dimensional world. I hope that you can live in that world, too, as your best self. Whatever the case, it will be an eccentric, courageous path that you must create!

A person who has given up all desires for sense gratification,
Who lives free from desires, who has
given up all sense of proprietorship
And is devoid of false ego – he alone can attain real peace.

—THE BHAGAVAD GITA

ACKNOWLEDGMENTS

I want to thank Robert and Kurt, my two husbands, for giving me the love and support I needed at different times in my life. Thank you to my children, biological and step, for expanding my tolerance and joy. I want to thank Sara for a beautiful friendship. Thank you to all the tutors who entered my life to work with my autistic children: Rachel, Kristin, Karly, Mona Lisa, Marti, Moses, Isaiah, Shane, Amanda, Josh, James, Shawnee, Derricka, Mike, Chris, Lydia, Priscilla, Mike, Melanie, Octavia, Tianecia and others. I want to thank all my EA friends. I know it's been said, but it *does* take a village!

Finally, thank you to Heather Desrocher and Kat Langenheim, my editors, for helping me put this book together and organize my thoughts!

ABOUT THE AUTHOR

Stacy Blemaster grew up in Shaker Heights, Ohio, received a BA from Brown University where she majored in theater. She then went on to be licensed in counseling and human services, earning an MA from John Carroll University. She has two autistic sons and a daughter, all now adults. She resides in Placida, Florida, with her husband Robert and their two Golden Retrievers, Libby and Lacey.

www.ingramcontent.com/pod-product-compliance
Lightning Source LLC
Chambersburg PA
CBHW061809070526
44586CB00024B/2767